Dear God, Thank You for NOT Answering My Prayer

Virtually all Scripture references are quoted from the King James
translation of the Holy Bible.

Dear God, Thank You For Not Answering My Prayer
Copyright ©2000 by Midnight Call Ministries
West Columbia, South Carolina 29170
Published by The Olive Press, a division of Midnight Call Ministries -
Columbia, SC 29228 U.S.A.

Copy typist:	Lynn Jeffcoat, Kathy Roland
Copy Editor:	Susanna Cancassi
Proofreaders:	Angie Peters, Susanna Cancassi
Layout/Design:	Michelle Kim
Lithography:	Simon Froese
Cover Design:	Michelle Kim

Library of Congress Cataloging-in-Publication Data

Froese, Arno - Steiger, Dieter
        Dear God, Thank You For Not Answering My Prayer
        ISBN #0-937422-51-7

        1. Bible Study/Christian Living/Devotional

Printed in the United States of America

Contents

11

INTRODUCTION

15

CHAPTER 1

Spirit, Soul And Body

The "Now" Generation • Dividing Soul And Spirit • The Two-Edged Sword • Word Of God As Discerner • "Soulish" Christians • Who Is A True Christian? • Spirit Against Flesh

25

CHAPTER 2

Unanswered Prayer

Jesus - Son Of God • Hours Of Darkness • The Sinless One • Why Me, Lord? • The Perfect Work • We Are Resurrected With Him • We Are In Heaven With Him • The Great Silent Answer • Before The Foundation Of

The World • Selfless Sacrifice • Lies At Funerals • Jesus In The Garden • Peter Failed • Gethsemane • Jesus' Continuous Prayer • The Agony • Gethsemane Temptation • Lamb To The Slaughter • Death At Gethsemane? • Born Once, Die Twice • When God Does Not Answer

45

CHAPTER 3

Fulfillment

That It May Be Fulfilled • John The Baptist • Pharisees And Sadducees • Prophecy Of The New Covenant • National Pride • The Baptism Of Jesus • Gentile Partakers • There Is Light In Darkness • The Temptation • Protection • Kingdoms Of The World • Jesus Subject To Rome • "No" To Sin • God's Protection • First Things First • John The Baptist In Prison • The Unannounced Birth • John In The Wilderness • Second Class Galilee • Seeing Is Not Always Believing

69

CHAPTER 4

Calling Of The Apostles

Follow Me • Two More Fishermen • The Election • No Repentance Required

CHAPTER 5

PETER: The Rock

Case Of Celebrity • Multiplication Of Food • The Wind Was Contrary • Endtime Picture • Peter Walks On Water • Danger Of Sign–Seekers • Peter's Confession • Today's Church • Rome's Church • The True Church • The Secret Messiah? •The Suffering Servant • Peter's Fall • Peter's Denial • Peter's Desperate Action •Peter's Breakdown • Peter The Fisherman • Jesus Stood At The Shore •Come And Dine • Peter's Love Questioned • Bondage Instead Of Freedom • Peter Leads • The Day Of Pentecost •The First Miracle • Filled With The Spirit •The First Conflict •"I Am Spirit-Filled" • Two Deceivers Exposed • Church Discipline • Salvation In Samaria • Dead Raised • Gentiles Receive Salvation •Resurrection Witness • The Keys Of Heaven • The Bible: Our Eternal Rock • The Bible: A Historical Book • The Bible: A Scientific Book • The Bible Says "Come" • Simple Salvation • Guideline To War

CHAPTER 6

MOSES: A Man Of God

Moses Meets God • The Eternal "I AM" •The Rod Of Moses •The Leprous Hand • Water Becomes Blood • Moses Believes God • Moses Responsible For Israel • Israel's Unbelief • Moses' Dialogue For Israel • Moses Defends God's Honor • Moses Seeks God's Presence • God's Glory And Moses

131

CHAPTER 7

JOB: Patient In Tribulation

Intercession In Vain? • "Dost Thou Still Retain Thine Integrity?" • A Compassionate Start • Accusations - The Wrong Continuation • What Did God Think Of Job's Friends? • Job Justified • Does Prayer Change God's Mind? • Not Against Flesh And Blood

141

CHAPTER 8

JONAH: Compassion Or Judgment?

Two Vastly Different Prayers • Israel, The Elder Son • "Doest Thou Well?" • The Paradoxical Prayer Of A Man Who Is Tired Of Life • The Convincing Comparison

149

CHAPTER 9

ELIJAH: Zealous For God And Israel

Elijah Vs. Ahab - God Or Baal? • Power In Prayer • Answer From Heaven • The Altar Of The Whole People • God Does Not Let Go Of His Servant • The Unanswered Prayer Cry • Whole Help • New Steps • Overcome By God • Inner Healing • Carried To Heaven Instead Of A Prophet's Tomb

CHAPTER 10

PAUL: *My Strength In Your Weakness*

The Preserving Blows • Three Prayers - No Deliverance • Suffering Teaches Us To Pray • The All-Sufficient Grace Of God • Of Good Courage • Europe In Focus • Church Growth • Guidance Through The Holy Spirit

CHAPTER 11

DAVID: *Lessons In Faith*

David's Youth • Much Resistance Before The Battle • David And The Giant Philistine • Religious Upbringing • The Anointing Of A Shepherd Boy • Special Training At The King's Court • The Fateful Error • The Consequence Of Self-Deception • Alone In The Valley Of Death? • Captain Over A Thousand • Saul Sets A Cunning Snare • Jonathan's Unique Friendship • What Is Our Relationship To Our Savior? • Voluntary Devotion • The Refugee In The School Of Suffering • The Prayer Of Growing Trust • Momentary Affliction • Inwardly In Great Danger • David Comes To Know His Homeland • Safety In A Foreign Country? • Flight From God •David's Kingship - Lessons In Leadership • Contact With Heaven • Beginning At Hebron • King Over Israel • Jerusalem Becomes The Capital • The Enemy Targets The Shepherds • The King Uses The Weapon Of Prayer • Grateful Retrospect • An Exemplary Testimony • Preparations For The Temple •

Nathan's Message In The Night • Fulfilled And
Unfulfilled Prophecy • Kingly Worship • The
Organization Of Worship • Song For Temple Dedication
• Singers Praise God • Inspired Building Plan •
Voluntary Collection • David's Greatest Fall •David's
Fall Took Place In Three Stages • Repentance And
Restoration • Chastening Grace • The Royal Psalmist •
The Heavens Declare The Glory Of God

217

CONCLUSION

Introduction

D oes God ignore certain prayer requests? We know that He hears the prayers of His people, but how many times have you brought certain petitions before the Lord and then, when the results you hoped for – even expected – did not occur, you became angry and assumed that God was disregarding you? How can you know whether your prayers align with God's will? What role does unconfessed sin play in communicating with God and in His response? These are some of the many thought-provoking questions we will explore throughout this book.

Prayer is one of the most important aspects of our Christian life, yet many of us become discouraged, disappointed and disheartened regarding the quality of our prayer lives. We may become angry when a prayer is not answered according to what we think we need. We may have no difficulty in proclaiming God's sovereignty to others, while personally finding it tough to accept that

God knows what is best. Often we may even find ourselves desperate and depressed, crying out to the Lord for deliverance…yet He seems to send none. What must we do? Rather than become upset or angry, we should evaluate the circumstances regarding our communion with God and meditate on His Word. First Corinthians 10:13 promises that God will not give us more than we can bear: *"There hath no temptation taken you but such as is common to man: but God is faithful, who will not suffer you to be tempted above that ye are able; but will with the temptation also make a way to escape, that ye may be able to bear it."* Unfortunately, when we feel like we are coming apart at the seams, and it appears that there is no way out, we find it much easier to focus on our surroundings than to saturate our minds with the many expressions of love and concern such as this that God reveals in His Word.

As we view this subject of unanswered prayer, we must look at two issues: first, whether our request is Bible-based, aligning with God's perfect plan for us; and second, whether we have prayed diligently enough. Too often we pray only once regarding certain situations and give up after a short time because we regard the lack of an immediate response as a signal that God is ignoring our request. Our prayers must graduate to the level of urgency! Prayer should illustrate an "I-can-do-nothing-without-You" attitude to the Lord. We show our complete reliance on Him when we pray. In essence, our prayers demonstrate that we believe without a shadow of a doubt that He is *"…able to do exceeding abundantly above all that we ask or think, according to the power that worketh in us"*

(Ephesians 3:20). If we give up after bringing our request before the Lord only a handful of times, then we must ask ourselves how important this request was in the first place.

While we should pray without ceasing (1st Thessalonians 5:17) and pray diligently and fervently, we must never forget that God is not a vending machine, nor is He a genie. He is Almighty God! For example, contrary to the teaching from certain pulpits, we cannot demand that God take away our debt in the name of Jesus; however, we can pray that the Lord would help us become better stewards of all that He has given to us. We cannot command the Lord to change our financial status; however, we can ask the Lord to *"give us this day our daily bread"* (Luke 11:3). See the difference? Which prayer do you think brings God the most glory?

You are about to enter into the lives of many great men of God who made requests of the Lord, requests that He chose to deny for His reason, His purpose, and ultimately His glory. You may identify with some of these circumstances, but what is more important, we pray that these character studies will help you better understand why some prayers are answered and others are not. You will also learn that it is more important to look at the big picture and see that the way things turn out is usually better than we expect! The content of *Dear God, Thank You for Not Answering My Prayer* will remind you that God's plans are perfect, while our idea of what we feel we need is imperfect. The Lord knows what is best for us, we need only trust Him.

It is our prayer that you will be encouraged, edified and exhorted as you continue to press on toward the goal for the prize of the upward call!

—Susanna Cancassi
The Olive Press

CHAPTER 1

Spirit, Soul, & Body

"My voice shalt thou hear in the morning, O LORD; in the morning will I direct my prayer unto thee, and will look up"

Psalm 5:3

"...the prayer of the upright is his delight."

Proverbs 15:8

There seems to be nothing more important to us than answers to our prayers. Not only does this apply to the public at large, but particularly to Christians. We want our needs met. We must have things now. Our sense of entitlement and instant gratification demands that we want what we want, when we want it.

Boldly we proclaim that Jesus is the Savior of the world; God is the Creator of heaven and earth, and based on the promises we have read in our Bible so many times, we know that He supplies all of our needs. His providence is inexhaustible. He is with us always; even to the end of the world. Therefore, we expect God to react positively to all of our petitions.

Not only do we expect God to take care of us and our family in a general sense, but we want more and we want it now! Although we are admonished to be patient, even *"patient in tribulation"* (Romans 12:12), it seems that we only have patience when we don't need it.

THE "NOW" GENERATION

The inspiration for such behavior is often blamed on our modern society. Today's culture expects everything to be ready immediately. The days of having to go to a tailor to have a suit made are long gone.

Car dealers highlight the fact that a brand new car is ready to drive off the lot today.

Even ready-made houses are offered for immediate occupancy.

Therefore, the reasons for our social behavior can conveniently be attributed to the progress of our modern society.

While such a development can be considered natural, the problem is that so many Christians transfer this behavior to their spiritual life. That is a great tragedy because our spiritual life should not depend on our social behavior, which is subject to our surroundings.

The enemy of our soul delights in this game of confusion. He tells us, "Look here, look there; see this, see that." Quite often, we willingly follow the devil's dictates and end up bound to the things of this world.

It is for that reason the Scripture emphatically warns us to seek the things which are above. In Paul's letter to the Corinthians the apostle wrote, *"While we look not at the things which are seen, but at the things which are not seen: for the things which are seen are temporal; but the things which are not seen are eternal"* (2nd Corinthians 4:18). Absolutely everything that we see, touch or possess belongs to the things of this world. Those things are temporal and will pass away, just as the entire world will. However, the things which are invisible in the spiritual realm will remain for eternity.

DIVIDING SOUL AND SPIRIT

One cannot deny that being spiritually minded is a lot easier said than done. Man is triune; consisting of a spirit, soul and body. When we are born again, our spirit is of God. We become eternal beings when we are regenerated.

The apostle Peter explained this in 1st Peter 1:23, *"Being born again, not of corruptible seed, but of incorruptible, by the word of God, which liveth and abideth for ever."* In the same way the Word of God lives and abides forever, so does our newborn spirit.

Peter continues his explanation by pointing out the difference between our born again spirit and our flesh, *"For all flesh is as grass, and all the glory of man as the flower of grass. The grass withereth, and the flower thereof falleth away"* (verse 24). Our bodies have no future because they are made of flesh and blood. No matter how much we pamper and take care of ourselves, this corruptible flesh is destined to perish.

While we may not consciously be aware of this process while we are young, we come face to face with this reality as we age. Our time on earth is numbered in days, hours, minutes, and seconds. In other words, our next heartbeat could be our last.

Peter also emphasized the difference between the Word of the Lord and man's body, *"But the word of the Lord endureth for ever"* (verse 25).

When our bodies become sick, the doctor explains the intricate functions of our organs so that we better understand how the prescribed medication is designed to fix certain problems we may have. We all want physical well being; we want to look and feel good. The volume of products available on the market to improve our insides and outsides proves our consumption with taking care of ourselves. If someone comes up with a phenomenal claim of inventing some unique new potion related to improving our health, he will peddle it to the millions. For example, weight loss is a huge and growing industry in the Western world. Astronomical claims and advertisements guarantee success beyond measure. Billions of dollars are spent every year with the sole intention of improving our looks.

The Bible confirms this when it says, *"For no man ever yet hated his own flesh; but nourisheth and cherisheth it, even as the Lord the church"* (Ephesians 5:29).

Renowned evangelist Dr. Ed Vallowe spoke at one of our conferences years ago and made a point of stressing how far we will go to take care of ourselves. He said, "Christians are quick to testify that they trust the Lord when it comes to sickness. But when that sickness has been diagnosed as cancer, then everybody, Christian or not, does everything in their power to get medical help. If you have cancer and someone on your block knows a physician who is a well-known specialist in that field, that Christian will not rest until he has given that doctor a chance to cure his terminal illness."

It is only natural that we take care of our "flesh" and make it last as long as possible. However, we find ourselves at a total loss when it comes to the spirit and soul. You can't go to a doctor for a checkup on your soul. The soul is the undefinable portion of man's personality which belongs to the spiritual realm. You cannot physically repair your soul, but there is a way to have your soul restored. Only when we open the Word of God will we begin to understand the reality and function of our soul and spirit.

THE TWO-EDGED SWORD

The Bible says, *"For the word of God is quick, and powerful, and sharper than any twoedged sword, piercing even to the dividing asunder of soul and spirit, and of the joints and marrow, and is a discerner of the thoughts and intents of the heart"* (Hebrews 4:12).

This is a clear guideline relating to our emotional lives which do not need the help of a doctor, psychologist or psychiatrist. It's only help is found in the Word of God, the "sharp two-edged sword" which divides the soul from the spirit.

This verse has become quite unpopular in these endtimes because we have progressed so far and have become so enlightened that we tend to venture outside the Word of God to solve the problems of our soul. Overbooked waiting rooms in the offices of psychotherapists lend sufficient proof that man indeed has a problem with his soul. What he is seeking as he sits in that waiting room, or opens that self-help book is a quick fix outside of the Word of God.

WORD OF GOD AS DISCERNER

Not only does the Word of God divide the soul from the spirit, but *"it is a discerner of the thoughts and intent of the heart."* When you immerse yourself in the Word of God, quite often you will find that the path you are on is the wrong one. Your intentions relating to your job or future may not be in your best interest or aligned with the Word of God. Your own way may prove to be successful for a while, but ultimately, it will end in great disappointment.

David, a man after God's own heart, knew the importance of His Word when he exclaimed, *"Thy word is a lamp unto my feet, and a light unto my path"* (Psalm 119:105).

"SOULISH" CHRISTIANS

What is the function of our soul? Contrary to our born again spirit, the soul is the indefinable portion of our personality which registers all that is earthly. The soul acts and depends on things that occur in our daily life. The soul rejoices to the heights of heaven when things go well, but is cast down to the depths of the pit when things are contrary to our liking.

Our emotions are the vehicles used to express the condition of our soul. If we rely on our soul, we are tossed to and fro due to various outside circumstances. For that reason, the Word of God divides the soul from the spirit.

Quite often, people confuse spiritual things with emotional things. We may call them "soulish" things. I am afraid there are many claiming to be a Christian who have never been born again, they have merely had an experience in their soul. They wept bitter tears at the moment of their "conversion," they can recall the exact day and hour of their emotional experience, but they never broke through to a living faith in the Lord Jesus Christ. As a result, they were never born again! The people whom I have just described are in extreme danger.

The greatest danger of the endtime is exposed by the

Lord with one word, "deception." If you faithfully attend church, support the work of the Gospel, and even attend prayer meetings, but are not born again of the Spirit of God, you have been deceived.

WHO IS A TRUE CHRISTIAN?

You may be asking yourself: "How it is possible to be a Christian and still be lost?" Careful reading of the Lord's words recorded in Matthew 7 attest to this great deception. In this passage, Jesus gave us a clear sign so that we may recognize whether rebirth has taken place or not, *"Ye shall know them by their fruits…by their fruits ye shall know them"* (verse 16,20).

Jesus exposed a group of "Christians" who had never been born again in verse 22, *"Many will say to me in that day, Lord, Lord, have we not prophesied in thy name? and in thy name have cast out devils? and in thy name done many wonderful works?"*

These people whom the Lord is referring are not Moslems, Jehovah's Witnesses, Hindus, Buddhists, or Mormons, because they do not recognize the Lord Jesus as God in the first place, nor do they believe that salvation is only attainable in the name of Jesus Christ.

The people we just read about in verse 22 are prophesying, casting out devils and doing many wonderful works all in the name of Jesus, yet the Lord's response is shocking, *"then will I profess unto them, I never knew you: depart from me, ye that work iniquity"* (verse 23).

Think about this scenario for a moment. A person who

has worked in the kingdom of God for most of his life may find himself standing before the Lord hearing these bone-chilling words, *"Depart from me, ye that work iniquity."*

If you are not 100% sure of your salvation, I implore you to make sure today. Seek the countenance of the Lord sincerely and honestly because the Lord Jesus promised, *"Him that cometh unto me, I will in no wise cast out."* Assurance of our salvation is an absolute must, *"These things have I written unto you that believe on the name of the Son of God; that ye may know that ye have eternal life, and that ye may believe on the name of the Son of God"* (1st John 5:13).

SPIRIT AGAINST FLESH

Not only does the spirit oppose the soul, but the spirit also stands in opposition to the flesh. Galatians 5:17 says, *"For the flesh lusteth against the Spirit, and the Spirit against the flesh: and these are contrary the one to the other: so that ye cannot do the things that ye would."* The Word of God confronts us with the real truth: the battle of faith. A person who is not born again of the Spirit, but has only experienced an emotional conversion, will have no interest in studying these important matters.

A "soulish" Christian depends on outward circumstances and notices what's wrong with this world. He will eagerly support the fight against corrupt politicians, homosexuals, crime, drug abuse, abortion, and other just causes. Most often to the point of fanaticism, he will oppose the evils of the world, with the exception of his own corrupt flesh.

As born again Christians we are most certainly against the above-mentioned evils, but the distinct difference is that as genuine Christians we present our petition directly to the throne of God in the name of Jesus, not on a soap box outside of an abortion clinic.

Throughout this book, we will look at how great men of God in the Old and New Testament acted in such a manner and experienced the greatest victory.

Galatians 5:19-21 provides a detailed list identifying the *"works of the flesh." "Now the works of the flesh are manifest, which are these; Adultery, fornication, uncleanness, lasciviousness, Idolatry, witchcraft, hatred, variance, emulations, wrath, strife, seditions, heresies, Envyings, murders, drunkenness, revellings, and such like: of the which I tell you before, as I have also told you in time past, that they which do such things shall not inherit the kingdom of God."*

The *"works of the flesh"* are followed by the *"fruit of the Spirit." "But the fruit of the Spirit is love, joy, peace, longsuffering, gentleness, goodness, faith, Meekness, temperance: against such there is no law"* (verses 22-23).

Here's the question: What is at work in your life right now, the *"works of the flesh"* or the *"fruit of the Spirit?"* When you become a Christian the Word of God separates the spirit, soul and flesh. Verse 24 continues, *"And they that are Christ's have crucified the flesh with the affections and lusts."*

CHAPTER 2

Unanswered Prayer

"And about the ninth hour Jesus cried with a loud voice saying, Eli, Eli, lama sabachthani? that is to say, My God, my God, why hast thou forsaken me?

Matthew 27:46

Now that we have laid the groundwork of our study, my personal question to you is, "What is your desire? What are you looking for? Is your future anchored on earth or is it assured in heaven for eternity?"

As indicated by the title of this book, we will attempt to reveal why God does not always answer our prayers.

Many instances in the Bible clearly show that God's silence was the best response. In other cases, answered prayer did not turn out to be the best thing for the one concerned.

One thing that we must always keep in mind is that God does things for His glory and our good. He is not a vending machine, and we cannot demand of Him to do what we feel is best for us. He is God; He knows what's best for us and if we remember that always, we will understand why He chooses not to answer certain prayers.

JESUS - SON OF GOD

We begin by looking at the most horrendous and shocking unanswered prayer in the history of mankind, *"My God, my God, why hast thou forsaken me?"* (Matthew 27:46).

This plea has such profound significance for all mankind. First of all, it reveals that God was indeed manifested in the flesh, *"...without controversy great is the mystery of godliness: God was manifest in the flesh..."* (1st Timothy 3:16). It further shows that in deed and in reality God became fully man, even subject to death. We read the following in Philippians 2:7-8, *"But made himself of no reputation, and took upon him the form of a servant, and was made in the likeness of men: And being found in fashion as a man, he humbled himself, and became obedient unto death, even the death of the cross."*

Jesus, the Son of God, left His habitation of power, authority and glory and became man in the flesh. We know from the Bible that He was tempted, tired, hungry and thirsty just as we are. He also expressed joy, sadness, displeasure and compassion, but there was one difference: He was without sin!

The most unexplainable mystery in the history of mankind was that God was manifested in the flesh. This simple statement has caused many to stumble because they were not seeking the truth.

Quite a number of today's religions do not believe that Jesus is the Son of God. Often they use this very sentence to justify their fallacy with the mocking statement, "If Jesus was God, then why did He pray, *'My God, my God, why hast thou forsaken me?'* Was He praying to Himself?"

Anybody who would dare ask such a question would quickly find the answer by studying the Scripture; and as a result, he would learn that Jesus was in fact God.

Let's take a look at some examples:

After Jesus healed a paralyzed man at the pool of Bethesda, His enemies made the following accusation, *"Therefore the Jews sought the more to kill him, because he not only had broken the sabbath, but said also that God was his Father, making himself equal with God"* (John 5:18).

They said that Jesus was *"equal with God."*

Those who mocked and accused Him testified to the fact that Jesus was God as recorded in Matthew 27:43, *"...for he said, I am the Son of God."*

When Jesus died, we read the testimony of an unnamed centurion in verse 54 , *"...Truly this was the Son of God."*

In John 20:28 we read, *"And Thomas answered and said unto him, My Lord and my God."*

HOURS OF DARKNESS

We will never fully comprehend what transpired during those dark hours on Calvary's cross. The Creator of all things suffered for His creation. The sinless One suffered for the sins of all mankind. The eternal life who became flesh, was poured out in His blood.

The Bible reports, *"...from the sixth hour there was darkness over all the land unto the ninth hour"* (Matthew 27:45). Undoubtedly, Satan and his demonic forces rejoiced, the hour of darkness had come; evil was no longer hindered by the penetrating light of the Son of God. Darkness covered the land for three hours. It seemed as though the prince of darkness had overcome the Prince of Light. At that moment, Jesus cried out, *"My God, my God, why hast thou forsaken me?"*

Jesus Christ, Son of God and Son of man came in the flesh, was debased to the lowest level of sinful man, and felt every bit of the pain, agony and God-forsakeness than anyone of us ever would. The Lord's cry to heaven pierced the darkness. This was, by far, the most legitimate prayer and most important question anyone has ever or will ever ask!

THE SINLESS ONE

We may all too easily overlook the fact that when Jesus prayed, *"My God, my God, why hast thou forsaken me?"* He was God-forsaken through absolutely no fault of His own. No one could have pointed a finger and said "He had it coming," or, "He received His just reward." Even the thief on the cross confessed, *"...we indeed justly; for we receive the due reward of our deeds: but this man hath done nothing amiss"* (Luke 23:41).

Before the cross, Jesus challenged His accuser, *"Which of you convinceth me of sin?"* (John 8:46).

If there had been sin in His life, you better believe His enemies would have pointed it out, but there was none.

Later, in Hebrews 4:15 we read, *"For we have not an high priest which cannot be touched with the feeling of our infirmities; but was in all points tempted like as we are, yet without sin."* Jesus was the perfect man, the perfect High Priest, and the perfect sacrifice which is why He can perfectly save even the worst of sinners.

At that moment, the universe witnessed the epitome of unrighteousness ever seen in all of eternity: Righteousness suffered for unrighteousness, the sinless for the sinner.

WHY ME, LORD?

How many times have we asked this question in desperation? "Why did that happen to my family? Why am I in such a predicament? Why must I physically suffer for so long? Why must I carry this burden alone?"

These are just a few examples of the thousands of other questions that have been exclaimed by generation upon generation. However, all the questions in the world, no matter how justified they may seem could ever compare to Jesus' question, *"My God, my God, why hast thou forsaken me?"*

THE PERFECT WORK

How did the Father in heaven answer Jesus' question? The eternal One answered His beloved with silence. Why? *"For God so loved the world, that he gave his only begotten Son, that whosoever believeth in him should not perish, but have everlasting life"* (John 3:16). Silence was the Creator's greatest answer to the heart-wrenching cry of God-forsakenness screamed from the lips of His only begotten Son.

When we dare to step into this holy realm and begin to understand this eternal, universal conflict, all of our problems, questions, heartaches and desperation become insignificant. The Son of God was forsaken by the Father for our sake so that we may have access to His presence for all eternity. He shed His blood to pay for our sins and died so that we can live forever.

Matthew 27:50 reports that in His dying moment,

"Jesus, when he had cried again with a loud voice, yielded up the ghost." John 19 documents the words that Jesus said, *"...It is finished: and he bowed his head, and gave up the ghost"* (verse 30). What is strange about this was the succession of events. When people die, they don't bow their heads first and then die; when life is taken away, people die and **then** bow their heads. This signifies the Lord's voluntary death on the cross.

What happened next is extraordinary, *"And, behold, the veil of the temple was rent in twain from the top to the bottom; and the earth did quake, and the rocks rent"* (Matthew 27:51). This is also very significant. The veil in the temple wasn't torn from the bottom to the top because in that case anybody could have done it. Instead, it was torn from top to bottom. God opened the way for sinful man to enter into His holy presence through the blood of Christ.

Praise God that the death of Jesus was not the end; He victoriously arose on the third day having fully paid the price for the sin of all man, for all times.

For almost 2,000 years, the invitation has been proclaimed throughout the world: *"Whosoever will, let him come and drink of the water of life freely."*

Whoever does come receives the Lord's guarantee, *"Him that cometh unto me, I shall in no wise cast out."*

Such amazing grace is completely incomprehensible to our natural being. We cannot fully understand that He who was sinless became sin for us and that He took our punishment upon Himself, obedient to death, even death on the cross.

Yet, in spirit we can grasp this overwhelmingly wonderful truth: Jesus died for me, purchasing my pardon; I am His possession, and I *"...am persuaded that He is able to keep that which I have committed unto Him against that day"* (2nd Timothy 1:12).

WE ARE RESURRECTED WITH HIM

As children of God, it is vitally important that we fully understand our position in God's kingdom. His unfathomable love is the driving force that makes His grace stoop to the lowest point of even the worst sinner, *"Even when we were dead in sins, hath quickened us together with Christ, (by grace ye are saved)"* (Ephesians 2:5).

Every person who puts his trust in the accomplished work of the Lord Jesus Christ has experienced a spiritual resurrection. We were dead in our trespasses and sins, but through Christ, we are resurrected to a new life!

As if that weren't enough, there is more! Not only did Jesus victoriously arise from the grave, but He also ascended into heaven and sits at the right hand of the Father. When we read the next verse we also find that this is true of our spirit, *"And hath raised us up together, and made us sit together in heavenly places in Christ Jesus"* (Ephesians 2:6). Notice that the past tense is used, *"He hath raised us up."* We already *"sit together in heavenly places in Christ Jesus."* What a glorious and wonderful position we are in! Notice that the word, "sit" is used. When does a person "sit"? Only after his work is done and his task has been completed!

WE ARE IN HEAVEN WITH HIM

The fact that we are in His presence in heaven today should motivate us to live a heavenly life on earth. Philippians 3:20 exclaims, *"For our conversation is in heaven; from whence also we look for the Saviour, the Lord Jesus Christ."* The Greek word for *"conversation"* is "politeuma" which, when translated into English we get the word "citizenship." This verse validates that earth is only a temporary dwelling. Our citizenship is in heaven with our Savior, Jesus Christ!

It is also important to mention that our salvation was one complete work. We don't earn our salvation in steps and, depending on our behavior, progress toward a certain goal. We are saved by grace, kept by grace, we walk in the presence of our Lord by grace, and we shall be changed by grace, *"Who shall change our vile body, that it may be fashioned like unto his glorious body, according to the working whereby he is able even to subdue all things unto himself"* (Philippians 3:21).

THE GREAT SILENT ANSWER

What would have happened if God had answered the Lord's cry? What would have happened if the Father had not forsaken the Son? What would have happened if God answered the challenges of the chief priest, scribes and elders when they said, *"He trusted in God; let him deliver him now, if he will have him: for he said, I am the Son of God"* (Matthew 27:43)? The answer is the horrifying reality of what we justly deserved! There would have been no salvation for mankind! Each one of us would remain dead in our trespasses and sins, forsaken by God for all eternity! Ephesians 2:12 makes our hopeless position frightfully clear, *"That at that time ye were without Christ, being aliens from the commonwealth of Israel, and strangers from the covenants of promise, having no hope, and without God in the world."*

If the Father in heaven had answered Jesus' prayer on the cross there would be no future for us, but an immeasurable, perpetual amount of suffering and an eternity in hell!

However, the Scripture continues, *"But now in Christ Jesus ye who sometimes were far off are made nigh by the blood of Christ"* (verse 13).

Therefore, the greatest answer to our Lord's cry for our sake, was His silence. Jesus deliberately came to earth for the sole purpose of redeeming fallen man. This was no accident or the result of any unforeseen circumstances; it was part of God's predestined eternal plan of salvation.

When we desire to gain a better understanding of God's ultimate sacrifice, we need to look into the reality of His intentions. We receive deeper knowledge in recognizing His eternal position when we occupy ourselves with His Word. Nothing happens by accident nor are there any coincidental occurrences with God. God is not dependent on our perception of time because He is timeless. When we have reached our eternal destination, we too shall experience that timelessness.

BEFORE THE FOUNDATION OF THE WORLD

Peter offers an expanded view regarding Christ's coming with the following words. *"But with the precious blood of Christ, as of a lamb without blemish and without spot: Who verily was foreordained before the foundation of the world, but was manifest in these last times for you"* (1st Peter 1:19- 20). Even before man had fallen into sin, God, in His foreknowledge ordained a plan of salvation which was manifested in these last days. Even the actual event that took place on earth was superseded by God's eternal resolution proclaimed in Revelation 13:8, *"...the Lamb slain from the foundation of the world."*

It is virtually impossible to grasp this tremendous truth with our limited intellect. How can something have occurred before it physically took place? We receive no answer when we ask the question on that level. Who can intellectually explain the Scripture, *"...he hath chosen us in him before the foundation of the world..."* (Ephesians 1:4)? We may only grasp this truth in spirit when we understand it from a heavenly perspective. To illustrate this fact, let's consider the following example: We know that the sun rises in the east and sets in the west. We can scientifically determine this through the use of instruments that measure the movement of the sun. However, this scientific fact would become worthless if we travelled into space because the rules change; the law of space would take over and we would see that the earth rotates on her own axis creating the illusion of the sun rising in the east and setting in the west.

SELFLESS SACRIFICE

To better understand Jesus' sacrifice, we must consider His complete willingness to give up His life. This fact is made clear in the gospel of John, *"I am the good shepherd: the good shepherd giveth his life for the sheep"* (John 10:11). Jesus identified Himself as the good shepherd, there is no other beside Him.

Further evidence of this admission is found in verse 15, *"As the Father knoweth me, even so know I the Father: and I lay down my life for the sheep."* Verses 17-18 reveal that He has the power to either surrender His life or keep it. It is completely up to Him, He is not forced to do anything. He may do what the Father has commanded, *"Therefore doth my Father love me, because I lay down my life, that I might take it again. No man taketh it from me, but I lay it down of myself. I have power to lay it down, and I have power to take it again. This commandment have I received of my Father"* (verses 17-18).

These verses are irrefutable; Jesus came voluntarily and willingly laid down His life, but because there was no sin in Him, death could not keep Him. The condemnation, *"The soul that sinneth, it shall die"* would have no effect on Him because He did not sin. What a wonderful Savior we serve!

LIES AT FUNERALS

During my lifetime, I have attended a number of ceremonies, funerals and memorial services. I often noticed that many lies are told at funerals. The person being buried was anything but a good and loving person, nor is he going to eternal glory because he died without Christ, he is a sinner condemned for all eternity. Often we hear this statement during the eulogies for military personnel, "These men and women laid down their lives for their country." What a gross exaggeration! The simple truth is that their life was taken from them by violence. Maybe they fought to their last breath with the hopes of clinging to life, but that doesn't change the fact that their life was taken from them. Jesus was the only One who voluntarily laid down His life and He did it for you and I!

JESUS IN THE GARDEN

In order to gain a better understanding of Jesus' voluntary death and the silence of His Father in answer to His prayer, we must first take a closer look at that fateful evening in the Garden of Gethsemane: *"Then cometh Jesus with them unto a place called Gethsemane, and saith unto the disciples, Sit ye here, while I go and pray yonder. And he took with him Peter and the two sons of Zebedee, and began to be sorrowful and very heavy. Then saith he unto them, My soul is exceeding sorrowful, even unto death: tarry ye here, and watch with me. And he went a little farther, and fell on his face, and prayed, saying, O my Father, if it be possible, let this cup pass from me: nevertheless not as I will, but as thou wilt"* (Matthew 26:36-39). From a human standpoint, this event is one of the most tragic in the New Testament. We read a detailed description of the Lord's behavior just before He was arrested, which led to His condemnation and final execution on the cross of Calvary.

Jesus took His closest disciples with Him of whom Peter was the foremost. Remember, just a short time ago, Peter had solemnly vowed to remain a faithful follower of Jesus, even if it cost him his life, *"Though I should die with thee, yet will I not deny thee..."* (verse 35). Peter made a very courageous statement by openly proclaiming that he would follow Jesus even if he had to lay down his life.

PETER FAILED

The Lord had already informed Peter that He had to die in order to fulfill the Scriptures. Peter understood this because prior to this event, it was Peter who identified the Lord to be *"the Christ, the Son of the living God."* Peter's admission occurred in a place called Caesarea Philippi where Jesus asked His disciples, *"Whom do men say that I the Son of man am?"* (Matthew 16:13). It is obvious that Peter was knowledgeable; he knew the prophetic Word had to be fulfilled. No longer did he stand in defense of Jesus but knew that death was inevitable. Notice that he said, *"Though I should die with thee...."* The fact that Jesus would have to die had finally sunk in, and now all that remained was the question of his remaining faithful to the Lord. Would Peter continue to be loyal to the Lord until the very end? According to the Word of God, we know that he did not. Peter denied the Lord, not once, not twice, but three times just as Jesus said he would.

GETHSEMANE

We now focus our attention on the Lord who travelled to a garden called Gethsemane, separating Himself from the disciples, accompanied by only Peter and the two sons of Zebedee. When He was alone a little while later, *"...he went a little farther, and fell on his face, and prayed..."* (verse 39). What was the content of His prayer? *"...O my Father, if it be possible, let this cup pass from me: nevertheless not as I will, but as thou wilt"* (verse 39). Jesus received no answer; again, the Father was silent. He walked back to His disciples, *"...and findeth them asleep, and saith unto Peter, What, could ye not watch with me one hour? Watch and pray, that ye enter not into temptation: the spirit indeed is willing, but the flesh is weak."* (verses 40-41). Something very natural had just taken place, the disciples' flesh was not willing or able to withstand the attacks of Satan.

We don't know how long the Lord prayed, but it must have been at least an hour based on this statement, *"What, could ye not watch with me one hour?"* Despite Peter's determined promise to die with the Lord, he had already separated himself from the battle taking place in Gethsemane.

JESUS' CONTINUOUS PRAYER

"He went away again the second time, and prayed, saying, O my Father, if this cup may not pass away from me, except I drink it, thy will be done" (verse 42). Again, there was no answer from the Father, only silence. Jesus gave the disciples one more chance, *"...he came and found them*

asleep again: for their eyes were heavy" (verse 43). This time, the Lord did not awaken them nor give them any instruction, instead we read, *"...he left them, and went away again, and prayed the third time, saying the same words"* (verse 44).

THE AGONY

When reading Mark's gospel account, we notice that the event is described with slightly different wording. However, Luke reveals that after Jesus prayed, *"...there appeared an angel unto him from heaven, strengthening him"* (Luke 22:43). The content of this strengthening is not revealed, but in the next verse we read that His prayer became even more desperate, *"And being in an agony he prayed more earnestly: and his sweat was as it were great drops of blood falling down to the ground"* (verse 44).

When analyzing this from a human perspective, it seems illogical because the previous verse said that He had just been strengthened by an angel from heaven, yet He continued to wrestle in prayer to such an extent that *"...great drops of blood"* fell to the ground. Was the strengthening by the angel an answer to His prayer or was this strengthening necessary so that He could continue to pray? I believe the latter was the case, as we will see when we examine this event in more detail.

GETHSEMANE TEMPTATION

It is commonly interpreted that Jesus, the Son of man

in flesh and blood was just as fearful of death as any other human being. Therefore, it is not surprising that Jesus prayed that *"this cup"* meaning death on the cross, would pass Him by. However, such an interpretation does not correspond with verses such as Psalm 40:7-8, *"Then said I, Lo, I come: in the volume of the book it is written of me, I delight to do thy will, O my God: yea, thy law is within my heart."* Jesus delighted to do the perfect will of God which was in His counsel before the foundation of the world.

To be certain that David was not speaking of himself in this passage, we find confirmation in Hebrews 10:7,9,10, *"Then said I, Lo, I come (in the volume of the book it is written of me,) to do thy will, O God."*

"Then said he, Lo, I come to do thy will, O God. He taketh away the first, that he may establish the second. By the which will we are sanctified through the offering of the body of Jesus Christ once for all." If we look at Jesus' prayer in the Garden of Gethsemane as a sign of weakness, despite the fact that He was strengthened by an angel, such behavior would contradict the prophetic passage we have just read.

LAMB TO THE SLAUGHTER

Consider Isaiah 53:3,5,7, *"He is despised and rejected of men; a man of sorrows, and acquainted with grief: and we hid as it were our faces from him; he was despised, and we esteemed him not."*

"But he was wounded for our transgressions, he was bruised for our iniquities: the chastisement of our peace was upon him; and with his stripes we are healed."

"He was oppressed, and he was afflicted, yet he opened not his mouth: he is brought as a lamb to the slaughter, and as a sheep before her shearers is dumb, so he openeth not his mouth."

Like a lamb, Jesus was led to the slaughter; like a sheep, He went silently.

DEATH AT GETHSEMANE?

These passages from Scripture give us reason to believe that something else had transpired in the Garden of Gethsemane when Jesus prayed that, *"this cup"* would pass from Him. It would have been an unnecessary prayer, an exhibition of weakness and undecidedness, but such a picture does not correspond with the overall description of the Messiah.

While on the surface the Father was silent to Jesus' three-fold prayer, the Scripture documents that His prayer was in fact answered. Hebrews 5:5 speaks of Christ as the priest after the order of Melchizedek, *"So also Christ glorified not himself to be made an high priest; but he that said unto him, Thou art my Son, to day have I begotten thee."*

Verse 7 contains the answer to His prayer, *"Who in the days of his flesh, when he had offered up prayers and supplications with strong crying and tears unto him that was able to save him from death, and was heard in that he feared."*

Gethsemane was the only place in which Jesus asked that His life be spared; Jesus did not die in the Garden of Gethsemane.

The apparent silence to His prayer in the Garden was,

as we have just seen, a clear answer to His prayer. From this point of view, we understand that Jesus' prayer was not that His life be spared on Calvary's cross, but that He would not die in the Garden of Gethsemane. Jesus was destined to die on Calvary's cross in order to take away the sins of the world!

What happened in the Garden of Gethsemane? From what we have read, it is quite apparent that the powers of darkness, even death, were ready to take the life of Jesus right then and there. In Matthew 26:38 we read, *"Then saith he unto them, My soul is exceeding sorrowful, even unto death: tarry ye here, and watch with me."* Mark 14:34 reveals, *"...My soul is exceeding sorrowful unto death...."*

Although Jesus did not die a physical death in the Garden of Gethsemane, He was certainly obedient to death; therefore, He tasted the two-fold death of a condemned sinner! He was *"obedient unto death, even the death of the cross"* (Philippians 2:8).

BORN ONCE, DIE TWICE

I believe we have a clear revelation that the Son of God had to die as a guilty sinner, not as one who pretended He was guilty. Jesus had to accept the punishment designed to come upon all sinners because the Bible says, *"the soul that sinneth it shall die."*

Many years ago, Midnight Call founder Dr. Wim Malgo wrote a tract entitled, "Born Once, Die Twice - Born Twice, Die Once." The message was directed to unbelievers who would have to die twice because they were born only once. But those who are reborn would only have to die once. The Bible says, *"...it is appointed unto men once to die, but after this the judgment"* (Hebrews 9:27).

If you are born again of the Spirit of God, then you have been born twice, and the judgment that would condemn you to the second death will not take place because it was already executed upon the Lord!

WHEN GOD DOES NOT ANSWER

This analysis of our Lord's prayer life before His crucifixion should teach us that the answers to our prayers may not always be decisive. We may experience defeat, sickness, tragedy and catastrophe. The most important thing to remember is that whether we live or die, we are Christ's.

I believe it is for that reason, when speaking of trials and tribulation, the apostle Peter triumphantly exclaimed, *"Wherein ye greatly rejoice, though now for a season, if need be, ye are in heaviness through manifold temptations. That the trial of your faith, being much more precious than of gold that perisheth, though it be tried with fire, might be found unto praise and honour and glory at the appearing of Jesus Christ"* (1st Peter 1:6-7).

CHAPTER 3

Fulfillment

"And she shall bring forth a son, and thou shalt call his name JESUS: for he shall save his people from their sins"

Matthew 1:21

Ve will highlight four important points in this chapter regarding the fact that Jesus gave little indication to Israel that He was in fact the promised Messiah. Four important issues that will be dealt with in length are:

1) His baptism
2) His temptation
3) His appearance in Galilee to the Gentiles
4) His proclamation, *"Repent for the kingdom of heaven is at hand."*

Before we begin this portion of our study, it is important to re-emphasize that nothing happens coincidentally or accidentally with the Lord. He deliberately and purposefully came to earth with the full intention of doing the Father's will. When we follow His life, actions, and sayings as they are revealed to us in the Holy Scripture, we must be mindful that He came to fulfill prophecy. We take special notice of this fact in Matthew's gospel account, where it is repeatedly stated that Jesus fulfilled the prophetic Word.

THAT IT MAY BE FULFILLED

Prior to Jesus' birth the angel of the Lord made the following proclamation to Mary's husband Joseph, *"And she shall bring forth a son, and thou shalt call his name JESUS: for he shall save his people from their sins"* (Matthew 1:21). This wasn't coincidental, it was the fulfillment of the prophetic Word as the next two verses attest, "*Now all this was done, that it might be fulfilled which was spoken of the Lord by the prophet, saying, Behold, a virgin shall be with child, and shall bring forth a son, and they shall call his name Emmanuel, which being interpreted is, God with us*" (verses 22-23).

Approximately 700 years prior to the birth of Christ, Micah prophesied that He would be born in the town of Bethlehem; "*But thou, Bethlehem Ephratah, though thou be little among the thousands of Judah, yet out of thee shall he come forth unto me that is to be ruler in Israel; whose goings forth have been from of old, from everlasting*" (Micah 5:2).

When King Herod issued his decree that all male children two years and younger were to be executed, Joseph, Mary, and the infant Jesus fled to the land of Egypt, "*And was there until the death of Herod: that it might be fulfilled which was spoken of the Lord by the prophet, saying, Out of Egypt have I called my son*" (Matthew 2:15).

When the children in Bethlehem were killed, we read the following in verse 17, "*Then was fulfilled that which was spoken by Jeremy the prophet....*" After Herod's death it was written, "*...he came and dwelt in a city called Nazareth: that it might be fulfilled which was spoken by the prophets, He shall be called a Nazarene*" (Matthew 2:23). When reading through our Bible, we notice that many Old Testament prophecies have been fulfilled and recorded in the New Testament.

JOHN THE BAPTIST

John the Baptist was the heralder who proclaimed the

Lord's coming. He challenged the crowds, *"Repent ye: for the kingdom of heaven is at hand"* (Matthew 3:2). John did not proclaim this message based on his own ideas. The message he spoke was in direct accordance with the fulfillment of prophecy as verse 3 confirms, *"For this is he that was spoken of by the prophet Esaias, saying, The voice of one crying in the wilderness, Prepare ye the way of the Lord, make his paths straight."*

John the Baptist was a rather strange character whose primary residence was the wilderness. The Bible offers this description, *"And the same John had his raiment of camel's hair, and a leathern girdle about his loins; and his meat was locusts and wild honey"* (verse 4). Undoubtedly those Israelites in Jerusalem must have recognized this to be a sign. Based on the prophetic Word, they knew that something was about to happen. John demonstrated this newness to the crowd by baptizing them in the Jordan River. *"And were baptized of him in Jordan, confessing their sins"* (Matthew 3:6). This was a prophetic illustration of that which was to come; namely, the Lord Jesus. They confessed their sins, sought forgiveness, and with a repentant attitude, they expressed their anticipation for the Messiah. The baptism in the waters of the Jordan demonstrate the expectation of the New Covenant.

PHARISEES AND SADDUCEES

It may be helpful to mention that the religious authorities–the Pharisees and Sadducees–had apparently recognized John's authority as well. Surely, they were impressed by this peculiar man who had separated himself from the things of the world so that he could proclaim the message of God in truth and with great authority.

He did not have to answer to a certain school or organization of intellectuals, nor did he have to answer to the official religious authorities in Jerusalem. Apparently, his words must have been impressive because we read, *"...many of the Pharisees and Sadducees come to his baptism..."* (verse 7).

John the Baptist knew of their intelligence regarding Scripture and the things of God, but he was not the slightest bit impressed. Actually, he used some very harsh words against them, *"...O generation of vipers, who hath warned you to flee from the wrath to come? Bring forth therefore fruits meet for repentance"* (Matthew 3:7-8). John didn't give them an opportunity to answer, *"And think not to say within yourselves, We have Abraham to our father: for I say unto you, that God is able of these stones to raise up children unto Abraham"* (verse 9). With those few words, John the Baptist exposed those living under the Old Covenant and its unending list of do's and don'ts, as ineffective for salvation. The Old Covenant was a broken covenant.

PROPHECY OF THE NEW COVENANT

Approximately 600 years before John the Baptist, Jeremiah the prophet proclaimed, *"Behold, the days come, saith the LORD, that I will make a new covenant with the house of Israel, and with the house of Judah"* (Jeremiah 31:31).

Then he explained the difference between the Old and New Covenant, *"Not according to the covenant that I made with their fathers in the day that I took them by the hand to bring them out of the land of Egypt; which my covenant they brake, although I was an husband unto them, saith the LORD: But this shall be the covenant that I will make with the house of Israel; After those days, saith the LORD, I will put my law in their inward parts, and write it in their hearts; and will be their God, and they shall be my people"* (verses 32-33). Notice that they broke the Old Covenant. When a contract or covenant is broken, it is invalidated. Thus, a New Covenant was to replace it, not one written in stone, but written in their hearts. When we read these words, we notice that part of this was already fulfilled; Jesus did come and establish the New Covenant sealed with His own blood on Calvary's cross, but the people of Israel did not receive this New Covenant as a nation. Verse 34 continues, *"And they shall teach no more every man his neighbour, and every man his brother, saying, Know the LORD: for they shall all know me, from the least of them unto the greatest of them, saith the LORD: for I will forgive their iniquity, and I will remember their sin no more."* Israel has a wonderful future ahead of them because this prophecy has not yet been fulfilled. Think about it: an entire nation will be saved. This is unprecedented in the history of salvation. Many books report revivals in various parts of the world, but such revivals have never resulted in the salvation of all people in that area. However, this promise will come into being for God's chosen people: Israel.

Someone may ask, "How is this possible?" Israel seems

to be drifting farther and farther away from the God of the Bible every day. Out of respect for their high calling, I will not list the terrible things that are currently taking place among the people of this land. So the question as to how they can be saved is not based on their seeking the Lord or keeping the law, but based solely on His grace, just as everyone of us has been saved. The foundation of their salvation is the great "I will" of the Lord Himself, "...*I will forgive their iniquity and I will remember their sin no more.*"

It is important to mention that this is speaking of a national, collective salvation of Israel, not on an individual basis. At this moment, reliable sources tell us that more and more Jewish people are coming to faith in Jesus as their Messiah. Those who believe and are born again are added to the Church and no longer belong to the category of those who will be saved at the appearance of the Lord in Israel on the Mount of Olives.

NATIONAL PRIDE

I believe that many of us would do well to examine our lives as far as the truth is concerned and discontinue our reliance on family tradition, heritage and nationality. The Pharisees and Sadducees had valid reasons to be proud. They were descendants of Abraham who received direct promises from God! What I am trying to get at is the fact that as Gentiles, we are nothing. In his letter to the church at Ephesus Paul wrote, "*That at that time ye were without Christ, being aliens from the commonwealth of Israel, and strangers from the covenants of promise, having no hope, and without God in the world"* (Ephesians 2:12). What a terrible position we were in. There is nothing worse than being hopeless, but that is exactly what we were. So any parading of our nationality, heritage, tradition, or family is nothing but vanity. As I already mentioned, Israel is the only one with a reason to be proud of their nationality, heritage, tradition, and family. Listen to the testimony of Paul the Jew, *"Though I might also have confidence in the flesh. If any other man thinketh that he hath whereof he might trust in the flesh, I more: Circumcised the eighth day, of the stock of Israel, of the tribe of Benjamin, an Hebrew of the Hebrews; as touching the law, a Pharisee; Concerning zeal, persecuting the church; touching the righteousness which is in the law, blameless. But what things were gain to me, those I counted loss for Christ. Yea doubtless, and I count all things but loss for the excellency of the knowledge of Christ Jesus my Lord: for whom I have suffered the loss of all things, and do count them but dung, that I may win Christ"* (Philippians 3:4-8). Therefore, as believers, particularly from among the Gentiles, if we have anything to be proud of in the proper sense of the word, then it is that we are sinners saved by grace. By the grace of God we have been chosen, *"That the Gentiles should be fellowheirs, and of the same body and partakers of his promise in Christ by the gospel"* (Ephesians 3:6).

THE BAPTISM OF JESUS

We will now carefully examine the testimony of John the Baptist, *"I indeed baptize you with water unto repentance: but he that cometh after me is mightier than I, whose shoes I am not worthy to bear: he shall baptize you with the Holy Ghost, and with fire"* (Matthew 3:11). John's complete humility in light of the coming Lord is exemplified in this passage of Scripture.

What was John talking about? The initiation of the rebirth and the implementation of the New Covenant that leads to perfection. In Hebrews 5:9 we read, *"And being made perfect, he became the author of eternal salvation unto all them that obey him."*

It is this Jesus, the "mightier one" who stood before John, *"...to be baptized of him."* John protested, *"...I have need to be baptized of thee, and comest thou to me? And Jesus answering said unto him, Suffer it to be so now: for thus it becometh us to fulfil all righteousness. Then he suffered him"* (verse 14-15). Why was Jesus baptized? *"To fulfil all righteousness."*

Jesus took on the human form of flesh and blood and followed the laws' requirement which stated that Israel should repent before the implementation of the New Covenant. Of course, in Jesus' case there was no need to repent because He was without sin. Nevertheless, the preparation was necessary and all "flesh" was admonished, *"...Prepare ye the way of the LORD, make straight in the desert a highway for our God. Every valley shall be exalted, and every mountain and hill shall be made low: and the crooked shall be made straight, and the rough places plain: And the glory of the LORD shall be revealed, and all flesh shall see it together: for the mouth of the LORD hath spoken it"* (Isaiah 40:3-5).

If John's prayer, (*"I have need to be baptized of thee"*) had been answered, and he had not baptized Jesus, the fulfillment of righteousness in this event would not have taken place.

What was heaven's reaction after Jesus was baptized? *"And Jesus, when he was baptized, went up straightway out of the water: and, lo, the heavens were opened unto him, and he saw the Spirit of God descending like a dove, and lighting upon him: And lo a voice from heaven, saying, This is my beloved Son, in whom I am well pleased"* (Matthew 3:16-17).

GENTILE PARTAKERS

As Christians from among the Gentiles, we should pay particular attention to Isaiah 42. A promise that God would bring judgment to the Gentiles is indicated in this passage of Scripture. Although He came for Israel, the prophetic Word clearly reveals that the Gentiles would benefit from His coming to Israel as well.

What a wonderful God we serve! He has not left us alone in darkness without any hope. We delight in the fact that He has given us hope. He has made the way of escape because the Creator loved His creation.

Let's take a look at a few verses from this amazing chapter, *"I the LORD have called thee in righteousness, and will hold thine hand, and will keep thee, and give thee for a covenant of the people, for a light of the Gentiles; To open the blind eyes, to bring out the prisoners from the prison, and them that sit in darkness out of the prison house. I am the LORD: that is my name: and my glory will I not give to another, neither my praise to graven images. Behold, the former things are come to pass, and new things do I declare: before they spring forth I tell you of them"* (Isaiah 42:6-9).

THERE IS LIGHT IN DARKNESS

Dear child of God, do you now see that your prayer to the heavenly Father need not be answered according to your wishes? John felt unworthy to baptize Jesus but he did so anyway, and as a result, a wonderful prophetic picture illustrating the past, present and future is revealed.

If you are burdened, dejected, and discouraged because your prayers have not been answered, remember that the Lord hears, sees, and knows. He will answer your prayer in His own way and at a time that He knows is best for you. You may be experiencing great difficulties to such an extent that you feel forsaken by God. That is exactly where God wants us. When everything has failed and you are disappointed, you have arrived at the point where the impossible becomes possible in and through the Lord Jesus Christ.

Often, I get the feeling that believers think they need to do something spectacular for the Lord in order to be considered a worthy servant. That is not the case because the greatest and most sensational thing you can do is recognize your own inability and let Him fill you with His presence so that you can fulfill your calling: to be a light in this dark world.

It is not decisive on what is being accomplished, but rather by who you are in Christ. Light does not need to do anything to attract attention, it is seen by all man. Jesus advises us of this in Matthew 5:15, *"Neither do men light a candle, and put it under a bushel, but on a candlestick; and it giveth light unto all that are in the house."* Quite naturally we would do the opposite. We are more inclined to show off our good works so that people recognize that we are living in the light. However, that is not the succession the Lord gave us, *"Let your light so shine...."* What is this light? It is the light of the Lord Jesus in our lives. By permitting this light to shine through our being, deeds, words, thoughts and actions men will, *"see your goods works"* and *"glorify your Father which is in heaven."*

THE TEMPTATION

"Then was Jesus led up of the spirit into the wilderness to be tempted of the devil. And when he had fasted forty days and forty nights, he was afterward an hungered" (Matthew 4:1-2). This occurred after the Father lovingly stated, *"This is my beloved Son in whom I am well pleased."* But now Jesus is led into the wilderness to be tempted.

The devil said, *"...If thou be the Son of God, command that these stones be made bread"* (Verse 3). Physical life is sustained by food. Although Jesus was hungry after fasting for 40 days and 40 nights, He clearly revealed that, *"...Man shall not live by bread alone, but by every word that proceedeth out of the mouth of God"* (verse 4). Jesus quoted Scripture in order to withstand the temptations of the devil.

Approximately 1,500 years prior to this event, Moses

made this statement to the Israelites, *"And he humbled thee, and suffered thee to hunger, and fed thee with manna, which thou knewest not, neither did thy fathers know; that he might make thee know that man doth not live by bread only, but by every word that proceedeth out of the mouth of the LORD doth man live"* (Deuteronomy 8:3). These words evidence the fact that our physical lives can and must become subject to our spiritual lives. The purpose of our physical life is that we have become new creatures in Christ and will live eternally. However, we can't become spiritual people unless we are physical people first.

PROTECTION

The next step in the devil's strategy to tempt Jesus was the misuse of the Word of God, *"...If thou be the Son of God, cast thyself down: for it is written, He shall give his angels charge concerning thee: and in their hands they shall bear thee up, lest at any time thou dash thy foot against a stone"* (Matthew 4:6). How clever! Satan manipulated God's Word. How did the Lord answer? *"...It is written again, Thou shalt not tempt the Lord thy God"* (verse 7).

KINGDOMS OF THE WORLD

The last temptation the devil presented during this incident bids us to take careful notice. *"Again, the devil taketh him up into an exceeding high mountain, and sheweth him all the kingdoms of the world, and the glory of them; And saith unto him, All these things will I give thee, if thou wilt fall down and worship me"* (Matthew 4:8-9). What becomes clear is that the devil owns all the kingdoms of the world. Bible readers know that all of the nations of the world are under the jurisdiction of Satan who is the god of this world.

Some theologians have said that this does not necessarily mean that the devil owns the nations but that he is merely presenting the Lord with a lie. This theology is based on the assumption that our nation (by whatever name) is not ruled by the devil because our principals are based upon the Scripture and we are God's country. That, of course, is wishful thinking because the Bible does not present any basis for such belief.

Jesus' reply to the devil was not, "You don't own all the kingdoms of the world," but, *"...Get thee hence, Satan: for it is written, Thou shalt worship the Lord thy God, and him only shalt thou serve"* (verse 10).

The devil's offer of all the kingdoms of the world revealed his true intention, which he will ultimately achieve, if only temporarily, through his inspiration of the Antichrist.

When we read Revelation chapter 13, we notice that the beast with the ten horns and ten crowns is the recipient of Satan's power, *"...The dragon* (the devil) *gave him his power, and his seat, and great authority"* (verse 2). We also notice that this beast, whom we call the Antichrist, becomes so powerful and popular that the world asks, *"...Who is like unto the beast? who is able to make war with him?"* (verse 4). This man is quite unique; he has attained so much power that no one can challenge him anymore. What is the purpose of it all? The answer is found in verse 8, *"And all that dwell upon the earth shall worship him...."* This is total dedication to the undisputed ruler of the world because he has received power and authority from the devil.

JESUS SUBJECT TO ROME

Because Jesus knew the prophetic Word, He did not argue with the devil, He simply told him what the Scriptures said. Jesus had no intention of changing the political structure of Israel, which at that time was under Roman occupation. Jesus said, *"My kingdom is not of this world"* which illustrates that He had separated Himself from the things of the world, but at the same time He was subject to the powers in existence which is evident from His statement, *"Render unto Caesar the things which are Caesars."* Surely He could have used other verses which would have justified any type of rebellion against the occupational forces of Rome, but He did not.

I believe that this is sufficient proof in clarifying our position as believers: Our task is to show forth the light of the Gospel, preaching it to all people, and making it clear to the Church in particular that Jesus will establish a righteous kingdom which no other form of government ever has or ever will!

"NO" TO SIN

If we analyze the devil's mind in this temptation, we

notice that he asked Jesus to do three things, *"Command that these stones be made bread"; "Cast thou thyself down"; "Fall down and worship me."*

I have read these events in the Gospel accounts so many times, but when I read them again for the preparation of this chapter, I realized what a wonderful Savior we have! Jesus simply said "No" to the devil and based His answer on the Word of God.

Dear brothers and sisters, are you asking God to turn stones into bread? Of course your first reaction might be to say no, but ask yourself this question in a different manner: Are your priorities targeted toward the things of this world? Are you only concerned with the here and now? Then you are asking the Lord to turn stones into bread. You are asking for the sustenance of your flesh and blood which has been given no promise and will not inherit eternal life.

GOD'S PROTECTION

Quite often I hear believers say, "The Lord always protects wonderfully" to which I reply, "Yes He does, but He doesn't have to." This truth was demonstrated to me recently in a letter I received from a dear sister who wrote the following: "My husband and I have served the Lord all of our lives and He has blessed us abundantly. After retiring, we enjoyed our golden years until recently when my husband was involved in a car accident. A drunk driver, with no insurance, demolished our car, put my husband in the hospital, and he is now in a wheelchair.

No need to mention the financial burden we had to carry. But that's not all. I too am writing, bound to a wheelchair because a few months after the accident, another car driven by a drunk driver without insurance hit my car, demolished it, and crippled me for life. Where is God's protection?" This heartbreaking letter clearly reminded me that God is not obligated to do as we think He should. Yes, He does protect and wants to protect, but He doesn't have to. I was able to comfort these two precious souls with the Word of God and the assurance that God does not make mistakes. Should He have apologized for allowing Job to go through such a horrendous turn of events? No, because in His foreknowledge, God knows what is best. One thing we can be sure of is that when we are in the presence of the Lord, we will thank Him for all the negative experiences, tragedies, and tribulation He led us through while we were on earth. The Bible says, "*...we must through much tribulation enter into the kingdom of God*" (Acts 14:22). James 5:10-11 says, "*Take, my brethren, the prophets, who have spoken in the name of the Lord, for an example of suffering affliction, and of patience. Behold, we count them happy which endure. Ye have heard of the patience of Job, and have seen the end of the Lord; that the Lord is very pitiful, and of tender mercy.*" The apostle Peter urges us, "*For this is thankworthy, if a man for conscience toward God endure grief, suffering wrongfully*" (1st Peter 2:19).

FIRST THINGS FIRST

After Jesus challenged the devil with the Word, "*...the*

devil leaveth him, and, behold, angels came and ministered unto him" (Matthew 4:11). If only we practiced this succession in our daily lives! It does not help much to ask the Lord to take away our difficulties, problems, burdens, distress, or even sickness. Some have made a "ministry" in capitalizing on the well-being of the flesh by holding "healing" services for those who are bodily afflicted. Many claim great miracles during such meetings without really knowing the purpose of it all.

The Bible gives very clear instruction regarding how we are to properly handle our physical infirmities, *"Is any sick among you? let him call for the elders of the church; and let them pray over him, anointing him with oil in the name of the Lord"* (James 5:14). That is the biblical way. You don't go to a "healing" service or to the pastor; you are instructed to call upon the elders of the church—which means that they come to you—and ask for prayer, *"And the prayer of faith shall save the sick, and the Lord shall raise him up..."* (James 5:15).

Isn't it better to simply follow what the Bible says regarding these things? In James 4:7 we read, *"...Resist the devil, and he will flee from you."* You don't have to fight or command Satan, all you have to do is say "No" to sin just as Jesus did; subsequently, the devil will flee from you.

JOHN THE BAPTIST IN PRISON

After fasting for 40 days and nights, withstanding temptation from the devil, and being strengthened by the angels, Jesus heard the terrible news that John was put in prison. Notice that Jesus didn't do anything to have John released, nor did He pray to the Father about it. Instead, He continued with His task, *"...leaving Nazareth, he came and dwelt in Capernaum, which is upon the sea coast, in the borders of Zabulon and Nephthalim"* (Matthew 4:13). Why? Because Scripture had to be fulfilled, *"That it might be fulfilled which was spoken by Esaias the prophet, saying, The land of Zabulon, and the land of Nephthalim, by the way of the sea, beyond Jordan, Galilee of the Gentiles"* (verses 14-15). Arriving in Galilee, Jesus picked up where John the Baptist left off proclaiming, *"...Repent: for the kingdom of heaven is at hand"* (verse 17). What a message! Remember, this is His kingdom; the perfect, heavenly eternal kingdom which was supposed to come on earth.

Jesus made it very clear during His ministry that this world was not His home, nor was His kingdom of this world, but that He was the King of the heavenly kingdom.

I suppose this was one of the reasons why the religious authorities, and the people in general did not understand or acknowledge the coming of the Lord. They obviously had preconceived ideas, knew history, and read the Scriptures, so it was no mystery to them that God had chosen them to be a special people on the face of the earth. They also read the prophets who spoke about the coming Messiah who would rule the world with a rod of iron. But Israel was occupied by Rome when Jesus was born and the Jews were only granted limited political rights and extended religious privileges.

It seemed only natural to assume that Israel would cast

off the yoke of foreign rule when the Messiah came. However, Jesus made no indication that He was heading in the direction of political liberty.

There are so many "missing" points in the life of Jesus that you can almost see some of the reasons why the people didn't believe in Him.

THE UNANNOUNCED BIRTH

Jesus was to be born of the house of David. Since David was a king, it would stand to reason that Jesus be born in a palace in Jerusalem.

His birth would have been announced and the religious authorities would have called for special festivities. A solemn assembly would have been formed and His birth would have been joyously proclaimed throughout the land, climaxing with a glorious temple service.

We know from the Bible that this is not the way that things turned out. The Bible simply reports that shepherds, watching over their flock in the field by night heard the angelic proclamation, *"...Fear not: for, behold I bring you good tidings of great joy, which shall be to all the people"* (Luke 2:10). To *"all people"?* Surely these shepherds outside the little town of Bethlehem were the least of the nation. Why wasn't Jesus' birth proclaimed in Jerusalem? Why not right there on the Temple Mount? This would have been a fantastic location for such an important announcement!

Just picture it: The heavens open, the glory of the Lord

shines upon the temple on Mount Moriah and the Israelites stand in awe of the supernatural appearance of the angelic host to announce the arrival of the Messiah. The Roman authorities would have understood and probably would have even respected the birth of this supernatural person.

Rome was religiously tolerant and would accommodate all types of beliefs. With a little bit of diplomacy Rome would have acknowledged Jesus as the new King of the Jews. But things didn't turn out like that. He came to His own, and His own received Him not. Even at His birth, there was no room for Him, Mary or Joseph even in the most common of lodgings. So, we see that there was no political, philosophical, cultural, traditional, or religious reason to suspect that this stranger, whom they called Jesus of Nazareth, should be the King of the Jews.

Nevertheless, this King of the kingdom of heaven who proclaimed, *"Repent, for the kingdom of heaven is at hand"* was in their midst.

JOHN IN THE WILDERNESS

Did Israel know about Isaiah's prophecies? Of course they did, but they didn't take John seriously when he proclaimed Jesus' coming. It is rather unusual that John did not choose Jerusalem as his platform to broadcast the coming King.

The Bible says, *"In those days came John the Baptist, preaching in the wilderness of Judaea"* (Matthew 3:1). John proclaimed the message of repentance in light of the kingdom of heaven being near, but he did not go to Jerusalem, the great city of the King.

During many of my trips to Israel I have seen areas of the Judaean desert. Based on the information I have on hand, there have been no significant archaeological discoveries indicating the existence of a mentionable civilization in the Judaean desert. Obviously, it was just what it says, a wilderness. Very few people go there, but we know from Scripture that Jews from all over the country came to this wilderness and were baptized in the Jordan River by John.

SECOND CLASS GALILEE

That was the situation in which Jesus appeared, worked, and fulfilled the task He was sent to do. After announcing the need for repentance, Jesus began calling His apostles. Again, Jesus did not go to Jerusalem, nor did He call upon the high priests to follow Him. Apparently, He had no connection with the Roman authorities. Instead of Jerusalem, He went to an unpopular place called Galilee. What was so bad about Galilee? Remember King Hiram of Tyre's reaction when King Solomon gave him *"twenty cities in the land of Galilee"*? The gift was not received well; in fact, his response to Solomon, recorded in 1st Kings 9:13 shows that he was rather insulted, *"...What cities are these which thou hast given me, my brother? And he called them the land of Cabul unto this day."* In the margin of my Bible, the word

"Cabul" is translated as "displeasing" or "dirty." Apparently those cities were still inhabited by a remnant of Canaanites.

Regardless of this Old Testament fact, this is where Jesus found His disciples, the men who would be entrusted with the message of the coming kingdom of heaven, *"And as ye go, preach, saying, The kingdom of heaven is at hand"* (Matthew 10:7). It seems as though Jesus deliberately did everything the wrong way. These men of Galilee were not highly-esteemed in the courts, schools or seminaries of Jerusalem.

When you look for top scientists, you don't go to a little country school somewhere in the sticks where people still draw water from a well, and electricity was introduced only a few decades ago. You will not find what you are looking for. In the United States, you would go to Yale, Harvard, or any of the other top colleges in the country to find a candidate that is worthy of your scientific undertaking, but Jesus chose Galilee.

SEEING IS NOT ALWAYS BELIEVING

We must always be mindful of the fact that what we know, see, and experience is not always decisive. As a matter of fact, it can be very dangerous and lead us into total darkness. In his second letter to the Corinthians, the apostle Paul said, *"While we look not at the things which are seen, but at the things which are not seen: for the things which are seen are temporal; but the things which are not seen are eternal"* (2nd Corinthians 4:18). Don't ever underestimate that seemingly insignificant person who loves Jesus and testifies that He is his Savior. Do not take for granted the little old lady in a wheelchair who is unable to take care of her basic human needs but believes on Jesus. And don't reject the uneducated ditch digger who doesn't seem to have any more brain capacity than to operate a pick and shovel but knows the Lord. These and other such people may very well be some of the Lord's greatest light-bearers. It may be that the greatest authors, preachers, and theological professors will one day look up to such an insignificant, but now glorious personality outshining everybody else.

CHAPTER 4

Calling Of The Apostles

"And he saith unto them, Follow me, and I will make you fishers of men"

Matthew 4:19

"And Jesus, walking by the sea of Galilee, saw two brethren, Simon called Peter, and Andrew his brother, casting a net into the sea: for they were fishers. And he saith unto them, Follow me, and I will make you fishers of men. And they straightway left their nets, and followed him. And going on from thence, he saw other two brethren, James the son of Zebedee, and John his brother, in a ship with Zebedee their father, mending their nets; and he called them. And they immediately left the ship and their father, and followed him"* (Matthew 4:18-22).

What type of person could qualify to be an ambassador for the highest King in the universe?

What kind of education was required in order to even be considered for such a high and exalted task? *"...Jesus, walking by the sea of Galilee, saw two brethren, Simon called Peter, and Andrew his brother, casting a net into the sea: for they were fishers"* (Matthew 4:18). If we analyzed this from a purely human perspective, we would have to admit that this was a mistake. The Lord shouldn't have called simple fishermen into such a significant service. At least a shepherd knows what he is doing; he takes care of his sheep, protects them as he is confronted with intruding animals, and always knows the number of his flock. On the other hand, fishers are wishful thinkers, their livelihood is based on hope, not on anything tangible. They cast their nets without knowing whether they will catch any fish or not. This is a happy-go-lucky trade. Even today's modern fishermen are distrusted in their testimony when talking about the big fish that, not surprisingly, always seems to get away. No fishermen in their right mind can say, "I will go out tonight and catch sixteen 4 lb. 3 oz bass." It simply cannot be done, there is no guarantee. He fishes with the hope of catching a fish and hopefully the fish will be big enough to take home so that he doesn't have to make up the story of the one that got away.

FOLLOW ME

In this Bible account, we read that Jesus used ten simple words to enlist Peter and Andrew into His service, *"Follow me, and I will make you fishers of men"* (verse 19). What was Peter and Andrew's reaction? *"...they straightway left their nets, and followed him"* (verse 20). With no arguments, no questions, no qualifications, and probably no education, they followed Him! They had one supremely important qualification; they didn't hesitate, they immediately dropped what they were doing and followed Him!

Jesus uses the same words to call you and I as well, *"Follow me, and I will make you fishers of men."* Are you willing to follow Him? When you follow Jesus, you immediately let go of everything else that hinders you from following Him wholeheartedly. That does not mean that you resign from your job. Leaving everything behind doesn't mean deserting your family. A husband or wife may not leave their spouses and children to go on the mission field. That would be a gross misuse of this command and a violation of the Scripture's instruction, *"But if any provide not for his own, and specially for those of his own house, he hath denied the faith, and is worse than an infidel"* (1st Timothy 5:8).

Spiritually speaking, the question is, "Are you really willing to leave everything behind, or is your deeper desire to look out for number one?" Would you rather get yourself into a good position for retirement so that you are able to afford this or that? Is your life on earth replacing what should be your first priority? Please remember that our lives are temporary. With each passing day we come closer to that unavoidable moment of truth when our lives will end. Where will your priorities be found?

TWO MORE FISHERMEN

James and John were also fishermen, and the next two to be called as disciples. How did they react? *"...they immediately left the ship and their father, and followed him"* (Matthew 4:22).

I wish that I had the ability to communicate the severity of your decision. You have two choices: you can either follow the world with all that it has to offer, or follow Jesus. The question is not whether you go to church, give your tithes and offerings, support a number of missionaries, or assist ministries in the proclamation of the Gospel. The question is, "Do you really want to follow Jesus **right now**?"

THE ELECTION

"And when he had called unto him his twelve disciples, he gave them power against unclean spirits, to cast them out,

and to heal all manner of sickness and all manner of disease. Now the names of the twelve apostles are these; The first, Simon, who is called Peter, and Andrew his brother; James the son of Zebedee, and John his brother; Philip, and Bartholomew; Thomas, and Matthew the publican; James the son of Alphaeus, and Lebbaeus, whose surname was Thaddaeus; Simon the Canaanite, and Judas Iscariot, who also betrayed him" (Matthew 10:1-4).

Based on the initial research I have done, there is none among the twelve who achieved anything extraordinary or occupied a great position in Israel's society.

Later, when Jesus fulfilled His task; died on Calvary's cross, was buried, arose, and ascended into heaven, the apostles, along with the other expectant believers experienced the outpouring of the Holy Spirit at Pentecost. It is recorded that when they preached the Gospel in Jerusalem some observers remarked, *"And they were all amazed and marvelled, saying one to another, Behold, are not all these which speak Galileans?"* (Acts 2:7). Their reaction gives further credence that the Galileans were not esteemed among the people in Jerusalem.

Obviously, their authority was not based on any intellectual status, but solely on the commission of the Lord, *"And as ye go, preach, saying, The kingdom of heaven is at hand"* (Matthew 10:7).

This message was exclusively directed to the house of Israel. Jesus commanded them, *"...Go not into the way of the Gentiles, and into any city of the Samaritans enter ye not. But go rather to the lost sheep of the house of Israel"* (Matthew 10:5-6).

NO REPENTANCE REQUIRED

Careful reading reveals that something was missing. Remember, John preached *"Repent ye, for the kingdom of heaven is at hand"* and Jesus proclaimed, *"Repent for the kingdom of heaven is at hand."* But in this case there is no mention of the word *"ye"*. Why not? Because judgment had already begun. Those who had ears would not hear and those who had eyes would not see and the ones who possessed understanding could not understand.

In Matthew 10:13-14 we read, *"And if the house be worthy, let your peace come upon it: but if it be not worthy, let your peace return to you. And whosoever shall not receive you, nor hear your words, when ye depart out of that house or city, shake off the dust of your feet."* The disciples were simply instructed to announce, *"the kingdom of heaven is at hand."* What we learn from this is that sin bears children. Israel did not expect His coming. They did not acknowledge His birth; therefore, they were not interested in His proclamation. The time had come that when the people heard the message they either believed or rejected it. That was their instruction. That was the proclamation of the kingdom of God for the people of Israel. However they didn't receive the kingdom because they rejected the King.

Many people in Israel did believe and when the time had come, their ears were open to the Gospel and received the truth. As a result, the Church began in Jerusalem and grew to Judaea, Samaria, and the outermost regions of the world.

Jesus is the truth, and the truth cannot be argued. You

will either believe what He says or you won't. Jesus doesn't need to present any special revelation or new scientific evidence proving that He is the Son of God. He has given us all the evidence we need revealed in His Word! *"He that believeth on the Son hath everlasting life: and he that believeth not the Son shall not see life; but the wrath of God abideth on him"* (John 3:36).

CHAPTER 5

Peter: The Rock

"He saith unto them, But whom say ye that I am? And Simon Peter answered and said, Thou art the Christ, the Son of the living God"

Matthew 16:15-16

We will now focus our attention on Peter, the first apostle chosen by Jesus. Although he was one of the twelve apostles, he was chosen by the Lord to initiate the Church in Jerusalem and the world. It is not surprising that Peter is mentioned in the Bible more often than John or any of the other apostles.

Therefore, it is important to take a closer look at Peter, the man who followed the Lord to the best of his ability. I believe that his later authority was partially due to the fact that he acted spontaneously. When Jesus called him and his brother Andrew they, *"...straightway left their nets and followed him."*

We mustn't fail to mention another person who acted spontaneously; Abraham, who is called the father of all who believe. When he was commanded, *"...Take now thy son, thine only son Isaac, whom thou lovest, and get thee into the land of Moriah; and offer him there for a burnt offering upon one of the mountains which I will tell thee of"* (Genesis 22:2). There was no debate, argument, or dialogue between him and his wife Sarah. Instead, verse 3 says that, *"...Abraham rose up early in the morning...."* We read of similar behavior from other great men of God throughout the Bible who did what God asked them to do right away.

It is unquestionably apparent that Peter was convinced that Jesus was the Son of God, the Messiah of Israel and Savior of the world. Peter's life is filled with examples of his willingness to follow Jesus without hesitation.

CASE OF CELEBRITY

After Jesus fed the *"...five thousand men, beside women and children"* (Matthew 14:21), He sent the disciples to the other side of the Sea of Galilee. This was obviously necessary because of the great miracle that had just occurred.

The people of Jesus' time were no different than we are today. When an important person makes an appearance, the masses will follow just to get a glimpse. If a politician, actor, or celebrity says something unusual, it usually makes the front page of the newspaper. Quite honestly, I find it comical that people who play sports are exalted by fans and the media as if they were a god.

Each year in the United States, we read what the President and his family have eaten for Thanksgiving. I cannot understand why people feel that this type of information is important. Apparently it must be newsworthy or the media wouldn't report it. Or would they?

In English speaking countries, the British royal family are always featured in some way or another. When the media promises an intimate revelation, people flock to buy the paper. This is a quite natural reaction and happens all over the world. Deep down in the heart of man, he is yearning for a leader, someone supernatural who could be classified as a god.

In the entertainment industry, the most outrageously imagined story receives the greatest acclaim. Fictional characters such as *Superman*, *Star Trek*, or the presently popular *Hercules* and *Xena* series are a smashing success because people want to escape into a world that is unrealistic, imaginary and fictitious.

MULTIPLICATION OF FOOD

A tremendous miracle had just taken place on the Sea of Galilee. Five loaves of bread and two fish were the only food available, but the Bible says, *"...they did all eat, and were filled..."* (Matthew 14:20). That was the miracle of multiplication. It is also significant that the Bible adds, *"...they took up of the fragments that remained twelve baskets full"* (verse 20). Some liberal theologians claim that Jesus must have hypnotized the masses and they all felt like they had eaten enough. Not only is this disgraceful hermeneutics, but they seem to overlook the fact that there was food left over.

Why did Jesus send the disciples away? Quite obviously it was to protect them from the possibility of being turned into a celebrity by the masses. The Bible records that Jesus *"...went up into a mountain apart to pray..."* (verse 23). What did He pray about? The Bible does not reveal the content of His prayer, but we can only assume that He prayed in relation to His desire to do the will of the Father and complete the work He was sent to do.

I am always amazed when I hear that some Christians think that prayer is secondary. Such thinking is extremely dangerous because prayer is nothing other than direct communication and fellowship with the Living God that must be kept, cultivated, and practiced continuously. God speaks to us when we read His Word, and we speak to Him when we pray. If Jesus Christ, who knew no sin, spent countless hours in prayer communicating with His Father in heaven, how much more should we be spending time in prayer?

THE WIND WAS CONTRARY

As Jesus prayed, the disciples sailed across the sea and were suddenly confronted with bad weather, *"But the ship was now in the midst of the sea, tossed with waves: for the wind was contrary"* (verse 24). That explains the reason why they didn't make it across in just an hour or so, but got stuck in the middle of the sea as they experienced this unexpected storm.

It is evident from the text that they must have spent a long time on the sea because verse 23 explains that after Jesus sent them away, *"...the evening was come."* In verse 25 we read, *"...in the fourth watch of the night Jesus went unto them, walking on the sea."* The fourth watch is the last watch of the night. It was the watch that broke into the daylight of the next morning.

Needless to say, the disciples were in great danger. The boats they used to cross the Sea of Galilee were relatively small and were at the mercy of the weather.

Suddenly, the disciples saw Jesus walking on the water but did not believe their eyes, *"...they were troubled, saying, It is a spirit; and they cried out for fear"* (verse 26). Jesus comforted them saying, *"Be of good cheer; it is I; be not afraid"* (verse 27).

ENDTIME PICTURE

I believe that this passage is a prophetic picture of the Rapture of the Church. As we already determined, the fourth watch was the last, as well as the most dangerous of the evening because the crew was very tired and not as alert.

In the parable of the ten virgins, we read that five were foolish and five were wise. The Bible says that before the bridegroom came, *"they all slept."* This spiritual sleep is now saturating the Church of Jesus Christ worldwide. If you have not noticed it yet, then you too may be asleep and in great danger.

The disciples, alone in a little ship on a dangerous sea clearly portrays the Church who is alone in the sea of the nations. Sure we can boast about various Christian activity, missionaries who are being sent to the field, the building of larger and more beautiful churches, a great number of radio and television stations and publishing houses. No one can deny that the Church is becoming more powerful and visible than it has ever been. But when we take a closer look at the Church, we must confess that true believers who stand on the Word of God are found few and far between.

I can well imagine that our loneliness will only increase in the not too distant future. After all, we are living in a modern, enlightened world where all opinions count and everyone is expected to be tolerant of the other.

We are considered naive, narrow-minded, and dogmatic when we preach, *"Neither is there salvation in any other: for there is none other name under heaven given among men, whereby we must be saved"* (Acts 4:12). We will find ourselves isolated, and in fear we will cry out to the Lord, but then Jesus comes alongside us and says, *"Be of good cheer: It is I, be not afraid."*

It is not surprising that Paul, under the inspiration of the Holy Spirit, concluded his detailed description of the Rapture with the following words, *"Wherefore comfort one another with these words"* (1st Thessalonians 4:18). What are these comforting words? That Jesus will come from heaven, *"...with a shout, with the voice of the archangel, and with the trump of God: and the dead in Christ shall rise first: Then we which are alive and remain shall be caught up together with them in the clouds, to meet the Lord in the air: and so shall we ever be with the Lord"* (1st Thessalonians 4:16-17).

Are you fearful, child of God? Rejoice and be of good cheer because with each passing day, we come closer to Him who is the answer to all of our fears and uncertainties.

PETER WALKS ON WATER

Although the disciples saw Jesus walking on the water, Peter acted spontaneously, *"And Peter answered him and said, Lord, if it be thou, bid me come unto thee on the water"* (verse 28). The Lord answered, *"Come."* This simple fisherman possessed a childlike faith and trusted in the Lord, *"...when Peter was come down out of the ship, he walked on the water, to go to Jesus"* (Matthew 14:29). What a feeling it must have been for Peter to walk on water! Peter's prayer was answered, he walked on water.

However, Peter's faith shifted when the reality of nature became visible. He took his eyes off of Jesus and focused on his surroundings, *"But when he saw the wind boisterous, he was afraid; and beginning to sink, he cried, saying, Lord, save me"* (verse 30).

Dear friends, seeing is not always believing, but believing is seeing reality. This miraculous event reconfirmed to the disciples that Jesus Christ was *"...the Son of God"* (verse 33). What was their reason for such a testimony? Once again they had witnessed a supernatural miracle that only God could perform. Surely they had read these passages of Scripture in the synagogue, *"He maketh the storm a calm, so that the waves thereof are still"* (Psalm 107:29). However, their confession was based on what they had seen and experienced. Because this confession was not based on faith, it did not remain. Later, we read that all forsook Him. Even when Jesus arose and the message of His resurrection was proclaimed, they did not believe. Why not? Because they did not actually see the resurrection, they only heard the report. Faith based on experience will only last until the next experience. On the other hand, faith based on the Word of God will remain eternally.

DANGER OF SIGN–SEEKERS

Matthew 16 begins with the religious authorities' vain attempt to provoke Jesus. They too wanted to see a sign so that they could believe. They were sign-seekers who received what they saw, and did not believe the message of love that God prepared before the foundation of the world. Therefore, Jesus warned His disciples against *"...the* doctrine of the Pharisees and of the Sadducees" (Matthew 16:12).

Based on the testimony that we read particularly in the Gospel accounts, virtually no one, including the religious authorities, could grasp the fact that Jesus was the Son of God. Then Jesus asked the disciples, *"...Whom do men say that I the Son of man am?"* (verse 13). *"And they said, Some say that thou art John the Baptist: some, Elias; and others, Jeremias, or one of the prophets"* (verse 14). It is obvious that the people recognized Jesus as a prophet; after all, He had publicly demonstrated that He was ordained to fulfill prophecy. No one could deny the testimony Jesus gave to His disciple John, *"The blind receive their sight, and the lame walk, the lepers are cleansed, and the deaf hear, the dead are raised up, and the poor have the gospel preached to them"* (Matthew 11:5).

PETER'S CONFESSION

But now Jesus goes one step further. This is very important because it is personal. Jesus, *"...said unto them, But whom say ye that I am?"* What others say or think does not matter when it comes to your own personal relationship with the Lord. Who do **you** say Jesus is? Is He your Savior?

When Jesus asked Peter who he thought He was, Peter confessed, *"...Thou art the Christ, the Son of the living God"* (Matthew 16:16). Immediately, Jesus revealed the source of Peter's confession, *"...Blessed are thou, Simon Barjona: for flesh and blood hath not revealed it unto thee, but my which is in heaven"* (verse 17). Peter spoke the words given through the Spirit by the Father. Jesus continued, *"And I say also unto thee, That thou art Peter, and upon this rock I will build my church; and the gates of hell shall not prevail against it"* (verse 18). Peter made the statement--Jesus revealed the statement, and on that statement, which is the Word of God given by the Father--Jesus builds His Church.

It is important that we understand that Peter is not the rock upon which Jesus said He would build His Church. Rather it is based on his confession (and ours) that Jesus is the Christ. That is the foundation on which the Church is built.

TODAY'S CHURCH

As the years go by, the majority of religious institutions are increasing in power, outreach, and importance. Who would have thought only 50 years ago that evangelical Christians would run state-of-the-art publishing houses producing millions of Christian books a year? It would have only been a dream to assume that Christian radio and television could literally circle the globe with the message of the Gospel 24 hours a day, 365 days a year. Today that dream is a reality.

ROME'S CHURCH

The pope of Rome is undoubtedly the most recognized leader of "Churchianity." When he came to the United

States in the beginning of 1999 requesting clemency for two condemned murderers, one in fact was pardoned.

Today, many political analysts agree that the pope's political crusade has contributed to the downfall of communism. After visiting Cuba, the doors for religion were suddenly opened. Even Christian holidays are now celebrated and endorsed by the Cuban government.

Billy Graham is recognized as a Christian evangelist around the world. In fact, he is probably acknowledged by more people than any politician.

I mention these facts to show that the infrastructure of Christianity within "Churchianity" is not necessarily the church Jesus said He would build.

THE TRUE CHURCH

Children of God who are born again of the Spirit can be found within various organizations and denominations. They alone constitute the true Church that Jesus is building, and against that Church *"...the gates of hell shall not prevail..."*

The true Church was not destroyed by the Romans, nor was it defeated throughout the many centuries that the political Catholic system ruled Europe.

The Church lived through Nazism and Communism, and the true Church will stand on Calvary's victory, even through the greatest storms of the endtimes when it seems almost impossible to exclusively rely on the Holy Scriptures. That is the Church, built upon the eternal Rock, the Word of God, which will abide forever.

THE SECRET MESSIAH?

Jesus instructed His disciples that they should, *"...tell no man that he was Jesus the Christ"* (verse 20). Doesn't this seem like a counter-productive instruction? After all, Jesus came so that He would be recognized as the Son of God, and all who received Him would obtain eternal life. However, in this case, He told His disciples not to proclaim that He was the Christ. Why? Because Jesus wanted the people to recognize Him through the Word. You cannot see Jesus in any church or religious gathering, you can only see Him through the Word of God. Therefore, Jesus is present wherever the Word of God is preached.

THE SUFFERING SERVANT

After instructing His disciples, Jesus revealed another side of His coming, *"From that time forth began Jesus to shew unto his disciples, how that he must go unto Jerusalem, and suffer many things of the elders and chief priests and scribes, and be killed, and be raised again the third day"* (verse 21). After saying these things, Peter again acted spontaneously. However, this time it was not in spirit, but in the flesh, *"Then Peter took him, and began to rebuke him, saying, Be it far from thee, Lord: this shall not be unto thee"* (verse 22). In reality, what Peter was saying is the message of today's bloodless New Age gospel. The Bible says, *"Without the shedding of blood, there is no remission of sin."*

The New Age gospel teaches its followers to think positive and that a high self-esteem is the key to success. There's no need to belabor this point; those who read the Bible know that self-esteem is not a virtue, it is a diabolically-inspired tendency to think more of one's own self than others. We know that Jesus preached just the opposite.

He said, *"...whosoever will be chief among you, let him be your servant"* (Matthew 20:27).

John the Baptist testified, *"I must decrease but He must increase."*

Under the inspiration of the Holy Spirit, the apostle Paul admonished the believer, *"...let each esteem other better than themselves"* (Philippians 2:3).

Self-love leads you away from Jesus and into the open arms of the father of lies, the devil.

The Bible makes it clear that we all love ourselves, *"For no man ever yet hated his own flesh, but nourisheth and cherisheth it, even as the Lord, the church."* Self-love is placing yourself before others, an attitude Jesus condemns.

PETER'S FALL

Peter, the first chosen apostle who had just made the profound statement, *"thou art the Christ, the Son of the living God"* now says no to the cross, *"...Be it far from thee, Lord: this shall not be unto thee"* (verse 22). What a contradiction! Peter had just spoken the wonderful words that Jesus was the Son of the Living God, but now he wanted Jesus to flee the cross. This is quite natural because we are incapable of pleasing God, nor do we seek Him while in our flesh.

Jesus said to Peter, *"...Get thee behind me, Satan: thou art an offence unto me: for thou savourest not the things that be of God, but those that be of men"* (verse 23).

Jesus did not answer Peter's prayer. He knew that the purpose of His coming was to fulfill the will of God. What a contrast from *"...Blessed art thou, Simon Barjona..."* to *"...Get thee behind me, Satan...."* With this statement, Jesus clearly and decidedly separated the things of God from the things of man. This statement also reveals that Satan was behind Peter's words.

Although the harsh rebuking Peter received from Jesus probably hurt him, it did not separate him from the Lord. He knew that Jesus was the Son of God, but in his flesh he simply could not grasp it.

PETER'S DENIAL

It was Peter who later made the seemingly convincing statement, *"Though all men shall be offended because of thee, yet will I never be offended"* (Matthew 26:33). However, when Jesus prophesied, *"...Verily I say unto thee, That this night, before the cock crow, thou shalt deny me thrice"* (verse 34), Peter defended himself again, *"...Though I should die with thee, yet will I not deny thee..."* (verse 35).

As the hours approached the moment of His arrest, Jesus went to the Garden of Gethsemane taking Peter, John, and James along with Him.

The greatest temptation of all time, which the three chosen disciples did not participate was about to occur, *"Then saith he unto them, My soul is exceeding sorrowful, even unto death: tarry ye here, and watch with me. And he went a little farther, and fell on his face, and prayed, saying, O my Father, if it be possible, let this cup pass from me: nevertheless not as I will, but as thou wilt"* (Matthew 26:38-39). Technically, Jesus was alone when He prayed to His Father as we see in the next verse. When Jesus came to His disciples He, *"...findeth them asleep, and saith unto Peter, What, could ye not watch with me one hour?"* (verse 40). In verse 41 Jesus reveals the secret between the spirit and the flesh, *"Watch and pray, that ye enter not into temptation: the spirit indeed is willing, but the flesh is weak."*

What happened in that Garden called Gethsemane? Was Jesus afraid of the cross? It is often interpreted in such a way, but that would contradict Scripture. In John 12:27 Jesus testified, *"Now is my soul troubled; and what shall I say? Father, save me from this hour: but for this cause came I unto this hour."* Jesus prayed to the Father that, *"this cup pass from me."* As stated in the beginning of this study Jesus' prayer was answered; He did not die in the Garden of Gethsemane, He was saved from death at that moment, as confirmed in Hebrews 5:7.

PETER'S DESPERATE ACTION

Jesus voluntarily went to the cross; nobody took His life, He laid it down and had the power to take it up again. Peter was there to defend the Lord when the mob came to arrest Him. The Bible says that he *"...drew his sword, and struck a servant of the high priest's, and smote off his ear"* (Matthew 26:51). We know it was typical for Peter to act impulsively. Jesus reminded him, *"Thinkest thou that I cannot now pray to my Father, and he shall presently give me more than twelve legions of angels?"* (verse 53). Why didn't Jesus ask the Father to send twelve legions of angels? Jesus answered this question Himself, *"But how then shall the scriptures be fulfilled, that thus it must be?"* (verse 54). The fulfillment is found in verse 56, *"But all this was done, that the scriptures of the prophets might be fulfilled. Then all the disciples forsook him, and fled."*

PETER'S BREAKDOWN

Although Peter had also departed, he secretly followed Jesus. However he was discovered by *"a damsel"* who *"...came unto him, saying, Thou also wast with Jesus of Galilee. But he denied before them all, saying, I know not what thou sayest"* (verses 69-70). It wasn't too long until somebody else accused: *"...This fellow was also with Jesus of Nazareth"* (verse 71). How did Peter react? *"And again he denied with an oath, I do not know the man"* (verse 72). The third time we read, *"...Surely thou also art one of them; for thy speech bewrayeth thee"* (verse 73). Peter wanted to remain hidden, *"Then began he to curse and to swear, saying, I know not the man..."* (verse 74). Jesus' prophecy is then brought to light, *"And immediately the cock crew."* Although he was quick to act and react, shamefully denying the Lord three times, we read of Peter's sorrow,

"...Peter remembered the word of Jesus, which said unto him, Before the cock crow, thou shalt deny me thrice. And he went out, and wept bitterly" (verse 75).

When we recognize our sin, failures and shortcomings, confess them and repent, we too weep bitterly. When we fail, our family can't help us, nor can our pastor or a psychologist. All it takes is a simple, truthful confession, "I have sinned" that holds the key to restoration. *"If we confess our sins, he is faithful and just to forgive us our sins, and to cleanse us from all unrighteousness"* (1st John 1:9).

PETER THE FISHERMAN

After Jesus was crucified, died, buried, arose on the third day, and was seen of His disciples, Peter returned to the Sea of Galilee. For approximately three years the disciples walked all over the land of Israel with the Lord. They experienced greatness beyond measure as the Lord raised the dead, healed the blind, the lame and the deaf, but now it was over. Peter went back to his old trade; fishing. *"Simon Peter saith unto them, I go a-fishing. They say unto him, We also go with thee. They went forth, and entered into a ship immediately; and that night they caught nothing"* (John 21:3). What a disappointment! They never hungered while they were with Jesus, somehow provisions had always been made. But now they were on their own again, doing what they did best; however, the result was devastating: *"...that night they caught nothing."*

JESUS STOOD AT THE SHORE

Scripture continues, *"But when the morning was now come, Jesus stood on the shore..."* (verse 4). He did not identify Himself but simply asked, *"...have ye any meat?"* (verse 5). The disciples replied, "No." After being out on the sea all night and not catching anything, it was time to give up. But then this unknown man said, *"...Cast the net on the right side of the ship...."* They did, and as a result, *"...they were not able to draw it for the multitude of fishes"* (verse 6).

Peter must have been deeply disappointed because even in spite this great miracle, he still did not recognize that it was Jesus who was standing at the shore. *"Therefore that disciple whom Jesus loved saith unto Peter, It is the Lord..."* (verse 7).

COME AND DINE

We now come to a very comforting and encouraging point in our study, *"Jesus saith unto them, Come and dine..."* (John 21:12). Despite their disappointment and fatigue they caught a large amount of fish, and when they came to the land Jesus invited them to, *"Come and dine."*

Often we make the mistake of thinking that all things, including the building of the Church, depend on us. Yes, we are commanded to work while it is day, going into all the world to preach the Gospel and to be ready servants of the Lord. However, if we carried the entire responsibility we would fail miserably. But even after we have worked all day and have not accomplished anything,

Jesus still invites us to *"Come and dine."* What a great God we serve!

Not only did He purchase us with His own blood and equipped us with His Spirit so that we can fulfill this task, but His compassion and love for each of us is far greater than we could ever imagine. The Lord continues to build His Church and has prepared a place for us as He promised.

In this case, on the shores of the Sea of Galilee, He had everything ready and was waiting with an invitation to His weary disciples to *"Come and dine."*

PETER'S LOVE QUESTIONED

The last intimate dialogue between the Lord and Peter is revealed in John's gospel account. *"So when they had dined, Jesus saith to Simon Peter, Simon, son of Jonas, lovest thou me more than these? He saith unto him, Yea, Lord; thou knowest that I love thee. He saith unto him, Feed my lambs. He saith to him again the second time, Simon, son of Jonas, lovest thou me? He saith unto him, Yea, Lord; thou knowest that I love thee. He saith unto him, Feed my sheep. He saith unto him the third time, Simon, son of Jonas, lovest thou me? Peter was grieved because he said unto him the third time, Lovest thou me? And he said unto him, Lord, thou knowest all things; thou knowest that I love thee. Jesus saith unto him, Feed my sheep"* (John 21:15-17).

These three beautiful verses express Jesus' genuine concern for Peter's love in an endearing way, but they also show the Lord's restoration. Remember, it was Peter who denied the Lord three times. Now Jesus asks Peter three times if he loves Him.

BONDAGE INSTEAD OF FREEDOM

Jesus made a stunning prophecy, *"Verily, verily, I say unto thee, When thou wast young, thou girdedst thyself, and walkedst whither thou wouldest: but when thou shalt be old, thou shalt stretch forth thy hands, and another shall gird thee, and carry thee whither thou wouldest not"* (verse 18). Certainly he was free to go wherever he wanted because he was an independent man. However, contrary to what we might expect, the future did not look glorious, but bleak; not new energy, but old; not free, but bond; not life, but death. This indicated that Peter's freedom in the flesh would cease. He would have to submit to the leading of the Spirit which is always contrary to the flesh.

I don't believe that the word "old" is limited by referring to the physical body, but primarily to the spiritual one, meaning that when Peter had reached a state of maturity in his discipleship with Jesus, someone else would take over, the leading of the Holy Spirit. This leading would send him to places and put him in situations he definitely would not want to be in while he was in the flesh.

These few verses make it clear that the Lord leads us to disregard circumstances and people. Peter was to learn that what counts is following Christ and Him alone.

PETER LEADS

At this point in our study, we have taken a look at the ups and downs in Peter's life, the prayers that went unanswered for his own good, and the many corrections he received directly from the Lord. Undoubtedly the words, *"Follow thou me"* must have penetrated his heart, soul, and mind beyond measure. Peter's later authority was established on the Lord's requirement, *"Lovest thou me more than these?"*

From the first chapter of Acts we see that Jesus commanded the disciples to wait in Jerusalem for the promise of the Father. Verse 5 states, *"...ye shall be baptized with the Holy Ghost not many days hence."* Thereafter, we read of Jesus' ascension into heaven. The disciples who witnessed the ascension are not named. The angels' message is very significant, *"...Ye men of Galilee, why stand ye gazing up into heaven? this same Jesus, which is taken up from you into heaven, shall so come in like manner as ye have seen him go into heaven"* (Acts 1:11). Not only did Jesus say that He would come again, but we also have the testimony of these two unidentified men who validate the fact that He will return the same way He ascended. In other words, instead of ascending to heaven from the Mount of Olives, He will come from heaven to the Mount of Olives.

THE DAY OF PENTECOST

Peter, along with approximately 120 other souls were waiting on the day of Pentecost, *"And suddenly there came a sound from heaven as of a rushing mighty wind, and it filled all the house where they were sitting. And there appeared unto them cloven tongues like as of fire, and it sat upon each of them. And they were all filled with the Holy Ghost, and began to speak with other tongues, as the Spirit gave them utterance"* (Acts 2:2-4). This was the birth of the Church of Jesus Christ.

From that point on Peter took a position of leadership, *"But Peter, standing up with the eleven, lifted up his voice, and said unto them, Ye men of Judaea, and all ye that dwell at Jerusalem, be this known unto you, and hearken to my words: For these are not drunken, as ye suppose, seeing it is but the third hour of the day. But this is that which was spoken by the prophet Joel"* (verse 14-16). Peter preached to the Jews in Jerusalem and as a result, *"...they that gladly received his word were baptized: and the same day there were added unto them about three thousand souls"* (verse 41).

THE FIRST MIRACLE

On their way to the temple, Peter and John were met by a lame man asking for donations at the gate of the temple called Beautiful, *"Who seeing Peter and John about to go into the temple asked an alms. And Peter, fastening his eyes upon him with John, said, Look on us. And he gave heed unto them, expecting to receive something of them. Then Peter said, Silver and gold have I none; but such as I have give I thee: In the name of Jesus Christ of Nazareth rise up and walk. And he took him by the right hand, and lifted him up: and immediately his feet and ankle bones received strength. And he leaping up stood, and walked, and entered with them into the temple, walking, and leaping, and praising God. And all the people saw him walking and praising God"* (Acts 3:3-9).

This poor lame man had prayed for financial support but his prayer wasn't answered. Instead, something much greater happened, the reason for his begging was removed. He was *"lame from his mother's womb."* This man was in bondage right from birth. Obviously, he had gotten used to it and was only concerned with life's basic necessities: food, clothing, and shelter.

It's rather amazing that *"...all the people saw him walking and praising God...and they were filled with wonder and amazement at that which had happened unto him"* (verses 9- 10). This should not have been. After all, Jesus ministered in Israel for three years and His fame regarding the mighty deeds and miracles He performed had spread abroad. Even the disciples were ordained by the Lord to *"Heal the sick, cleanse the lepers, raise the dead, cast out devils..."* (Matthew 10:8). In Luke 10:17 we read, *"And the seventy returned again with joy, saying, Lord, even the devils are subject unto us through thy name."* Tremendous miracles had occurred in the land of Israel during those three years, so what was the big deal? Why were they *"filled with wonder and amazement?"*

As I mentioned earlier, they were amazed by these miracles because their hearts were hardened and they lived from one miracle to the next. They could only comprehend what they saw, but that visible experience was only temporary. Their ears were deaf to the Gospel and their eyes were blind to the reality of Bible prophecy fulfillment. Scripture doesn't say that Peter and John were filled with wonder and amazement, but that the people were.

FILLED WITH THE SPIRIT

The imitation of the Church took place outside of the official religious institution, *"...the priests, and the captain of the temple, and the Sadducees, came upon them, Being grieved that they taught the people, and preached through Jesus the resurrection from the dead. And they laid hands on them, and put them in hold unto the next day: for it was now eventide"* (Acts 4:1-3). This appears to be an extreme case of jealousy. These educated individuals couldn't understand how ignorant people such as Peter and John could preach the Gospel and have the masses flock to hear them. Verse 13 confirms this point, *"Now when they saw the boldness of Peter and John, and perceived that they were unlearned and ignorant men, they marvelled; and they took knowledge of them, that they had been with Jesus."*

The religious authorities were powerless, *"...What shall we do to these men? for that indeed a notable miracle hath been done by them is manifest to all them that dwell in Jerusalem; and we cannot deny it. But that it spread no further among the people, let us straitly threaten them, that they speak henceforth to no man in this name. And they called them, and commanded them not to speak at all nor teach in the name of Jesus"* (verses 16-18).

THE FIRST CONFLICT

The disciples and the Church had a real problem on their hands; it was now forbidden to preach the name of Jesus, so the Church gathered for a prayer meeting. It is significant that this prayer meeting clearly revealed the Church's jurisdiction. Here is how they prayed, *"The kings of the earth stood up, and the rulers were gathered together against the Lord, and against his Christ. For of a truth against thy holy child Jesus, whom thou hast anointed, both Herod, and Pontius Pilate, with the Gentiles, and the people of Israel, were gathered together, For to do whatsoever thy hand and thy counsel determined before to be done. And now, Lord, behold their threatenings: and grant unto thy servants, that with all boldness they may speak thy word"* (Acts 4:26-29). This is an amazing prayer. They could have prayed for a favorable government; a "God-fearing" President; a "Bible-believing" Congress; or a "God-honoring" Supreme Court, but they did not.

The Church presented their case directly to God. Their prayer revealed that the opposition of the government and the religious institution was not against them, but *"against the Lord"*; *"against His Christ"*; and *"against thy holy child Jesus."*

They listed the people responsible: King Herod who was a half-Jew, Pontius Pilate the representative of the Roman authorities, the Gentiles, and lastly, *"the people of Israel."*

Notice their direct prayer concern, *"grant unto thy servants, that with all boldness they may speak thy word."* The answer to this prayer is found in verse 31, *"And when they had prayed, the place was shaken where they were assembled together; and they were all filled with the Holy Ghost, and they spake the word of God with boldness."* In other words, they were filled with the Holy Spirit. These believers had already received the baptism of the Spirit when they believed on the Lord Jesus Christ, but now they were filled with the Spirit. The filling of the Spirit must take place repeatedly. When does it happen? When we are completely empty of ourselves, when all is lost, hopeless, and our very calling is in question, it is then that the filling takes place. As long as we are filled with self, our ambition, plans and self-esteem, there is no room for the filling of the Spirit.

"I AM SPIRIT-FILLED"

It is also important to mention that people who were filled with the Spirit never made that statement themselves. Quite often, I receive letters from believers who make it a point of mentioning that they are "Spirit-filled." Usually these letters reveal that the person concerned is filled with everything but the Spirit!

The authority of the Church was clear; there was no protest, no political activity or marches, just a simple, sincere, direct prayer, "Lord, you commanded us to proclaim the Gospel in the name of Jesus, but now we are forbidden, Lord, help!" As a result of the Church's prayer, the members were filled with the Holy Spirit, and the Gospel was preached: *"...with great power gave the apostles witness of the resurrection of the Lord Jesus: and great grace was upon them all"* (verse 33).

TWO DECEIVERS EXPOSED

The story recorded in Acts 5 should be familiar to all who read their Bible. Ananias and his wife Sapphira had sold some property and kept back part of the price for themselves. They came to the Church and laid their money at the feet of the apostles showing off their dedication. Satan was victorious as a result of their pride, *"...Peter said, Ananias, why hath Satan filled thine heart to lie to the Holy Ghost, and to keep back part of the price of the land? Whiles it remained, was it not thine own? and after it was sold, was it not in thine own power? why hast thou conceived this thing in thine heart? thou hast not lied unto men, but unto God"* (verses 3-4). In this passage, Peter revealed that private property is to be respected. We may buy and sell, and we may choose to give or not give, but hypocracy is not tolerated, *"And Ananias hearing these words fell down, and gave up the ghost: and great fear came on all them that heard these things"* (verse 5).

CHURCH DISCIPLINE

The sinful act of Ananias and Sapphira led to the institution of church discipline. The spirit of judgment has been present in the Church from the beginning.

Often I read about certain groups who are attempting to recreate the original Church as it was in Jerusalem which, of course, is an unworthy goal. The Church is pictured as a spiritual temple. The foundations are laid, the structure is built, and the complete canon of Scripture has been given to us. It is my personal opinion that the last stone will be added at any moment and the spiritual temple will be complete. The result is the removal of the Holy Spirit who dwells in that temple, an event known as the Rapture of the Church.

I am not impressed when people tell me that they are duplicating the events of the early Church including the signs and wonders that took place in Jerusalem. I am not impressed because lies and hypocracy are not being exposed in the Church today. Why not? Because the spirit of judgment is no longer present in the Church as it was during the times of the apostles. This is evidenced in the Acts of the Apostles and the epistles to the churches written primarily by the apostle Paul. We notice that the spirit of judgment was no longer present in the Church even during Paul's time and much sin was simply tolerated.

In our churches, we wholeheartedly sing, "All to Jesus I surrender, all to Him I give...." But what happens if we don't really mean it? I believe you will agree that many of us are guilty of simply going through the motions and not giving it a second thought. Does anyone drop dead? Is anyone judged as was the case with Ananias and Sapphira?

What this event resulted in was the separation of genuine and nominal Christians in Jerusalem during the times of the apostles. Those who were not serious about following Jesus were removed. *"And of the rest durst no* man join himself to them: but the people magnified them" (verse 13). In spite of the separation verse 14 says, "*And believers were the more added to the Lord, multitudes both of men and women.*"

SALVATION IN SAMARIA

"*Now when the apostles which were at Jerusalem heard that Samaria had received the word of God, they sent unto them Peter and John. Who, when they were come down, prayed for them, that they might receive the Holy Ghost: (For as yet he was fallen upon none of them: only they were baptized in the name of the Lord Jesus.) Then laid they their hands on them, and they received the Holy Ghost*" (Acts 8:14-17). Something strange occurred because Philip preached the Gospel, the Samaritans accepted the message and were baptized in the name of Jesus, but they had not received the Holy Spirit. Why not? Because Peter was ordained to initiate the Church, not only in Jerusalem, but Samaria and the outermost regions of the world. For that reason, the Church sent Peter and John and the Samaritans received the Holy Spirit as well.

DEAD RAISED

Not only was Peter ordained to perform the first miracle in the Church, but he was also the first to demonstrate the resurrection power of Jesus, "*Now there was at Joppa a certain disciple named Tabitha, which by interpretation is called Dorcas: this woman was full of good works and almsdeeds which she did. And it came to pass in those days, that she was sick, and died: whom when they had washed, they laid her in an upper chamber. And forasmuch as Lydda was nigh to Joppa, and the disciples had heard that Peter was there, they sent unto him two men, desiring him that he would not delay to come to them. Then Peter arose and went with them. When he was come, they brought him into the upper chamber: and all the widows stood by him weeping, and shewing the coats and garments which Dorcas made, while she was with them. But Peter put them all forth, and kneeled down, and prayed; and turning him to the body said, Tabitha, arise. And she opened her eyes: and when she saw Peter, she sat up. And he gave her his hand, and lifted her up, and when he had called the saints and widows, presented her alive"* (Acts 9:36-41).

GENTILES RECEIVE SALVATION

Although Peter and the disciples clearly heard the Lord's instruction to preach the Gospel in Jerusalem, Samaria, and the outermost regions of the world, Peter was still a Jew who was true to the Jews and the Law. It was unthinkable that Peter would act like a Gentile by ignoring the dietary laws and not keeping the Sabbath. Therefore, in order to open the door for the Gentile, God led Peter through a remarkable experience in which he would clearly understand that the Gospel of salvation should be presented to all people everywhere.

We read the following account in Acts 10:9-16, *"...Peter went up upon the housetop to pray about the sixth hour: And he became very hungry, and would have eaten: but while they made ready, he fell into a trance, And saw heaven opened, and a certain vessel descending unto him, as it had been a great sheet knit at the four corners, and let down to the earth: Wherein were all manner of fourfooted beasts of the earth, and wild beasts, and creeping things, and fowls of the air. And there came a voice to him, Rise, Peter; kill, and eat. But Peter said, Not so, Lord; for I have never eaten any thing that is common or unclean. And the voice spake unto him again the second time, What God hath cleansed, that call not thou common. This was done thrice: and the vessel was received up again into heaven."* Three times the Lord showed Peter that salvation would now to be offered to all people all over the world. This remarkable event had barely passed when the reason for it became evident, *"While Peter thought on the vision, the Spirit said unto him, Behold, three men seek thee. Arise therefore, and get thee down, and go with them, doubting nothing: for I have sent them"* (verses 19-20). What did these three men want? *"...they said, Cornelius the centurion, a just man, and one that feareth God, and of good report among all the nation of the Jews, was warned from God by an holy angel to send for thee into his house, and to hear words of thee"* (verse 22). Peter accepted the invitation, *"And the morrow after they entered into Caesarea. And Cornelius waited for them, and had called together his kinsmen and near friends. And as Peter was coming in, Cornelius met him, and fell down at his feet, and worshipped him. But Peter took him up, saying, Stand up; I myself also am a man"* (verses 24-26). At that point, Peter preached the Gospel, *"While Peter yet spake* these words, the Holy Ghost fell on all them which heard the word. And they of the circumcision which believed were astonished, as many as came with Peter, because that on the Gentiles also was poured out the gift of the Holy Ghost"* (verses 44-45).

RESURRECTION WITNESS

It is also significant that the Bible emphasizes Peter's preeminence in relation to the resurrection witness. We know that on the first day of the week, Mary Magdalene and "the other Mary" went to Jesus' burial place. Because they were the first witnesses of the empty tomb, they experienced this remarkable event by hearing the resurrection message directly from the angel, *"And the angel answered and said unto the women, Fear not ye: for I know that ye seek Jesus, which was crucified. He is not here: for he is risen, as he said. Come, see the place where the Lord lay"* (Matthew 28:5-6).

What did they do? They ran to Peter and told him about the resurrection of the Lord. In an effort to convince themselves, Peter and John, *"...ran both together: and the other disciple did outrun Peter, and came first to the sepulchre. And he stooping down, and looking in, saw the linen clothes lying; yet went he not in. Then cometh Simon Peter following him, and went into the sepulchre, and seeth the linen clothes lie, And the napkin, that was about his head, not lying with the linen clothes, but wrapped together in a place by itself"* (John 20:4-7). John arrived at the tomb first. Although he did look inside, he waited for Peter to get there and confirm the resurrection by entering the sepulchre first. Continuing in verse 8 we read, *"Then went in also that other disciple, which came first to the sepulchre, and he saw, and believed."*

Later, when defending the doctrine of the resurrection, the apostle Paul named Peter first, *"And that he was buried, and that he rose again the third day according to the scriptures: And that he was seen of Cephas, then of the twelve: After that, he was seen of above five hundred brethren at once; of whom the greater part remain unto this present, but some are fallen asleep. After that, he was seen of James; then of all the apostles. And last of all he was seen of me also, as of one born out of due time. For I am the least of the apostles, that am not meet to be called an apostle, because I persecuted the church of God"* (1st Corinthians 15:4-9).

THE KEYS OF HEAVEN

The few events we have studied clearly reveal Peter's position of authority. The Bible is an open book and does not fail to include the positive with the negative, success with failure and victory with defeat.

With these many documentations in mind, we turn to Matthew 16:18-19, *"And I say also unto thee, That thou art Peter, and upon this rock I will build my church; and the gates of hell shall not prevail against it. And I will give unto thee the keys of the kingdom of heaven: and whatsoever thou shalt bind on earth shall be bound in heaven: and whatsoever thou shalt loose on earth shall be loosed in heaven."* We already determined that this

"Rock" described in Matthew 16 was Peter's confession based on the Word of God, *"Thou art the Christ, the Son of the living God."* This "Rock" is the precious stone which was rejected by the builder, but has become the cornerstone. It is the foundation upon which the Church is built, *"For other foundation can no man lay than that is laid, which is Jesus Christ"* (1st Corinthians 3:11). If the Church was built on Peter, it would have been built on a sinner. Jesus was fully God and fully man, He was perfect and without sin, and He is the foundation of His Church!

The literal, physical origin of the Church was only accomplished **through** a vessel; Peter. He indeed had the key to salvation when he proclaimed the Gospel to the Jews in Jerusalem, Samaria, and ultimately the Gentiles.

But Peter was a man just like you and me, subject to all the limitations of man and, as we have seen throughout this study, he failed many times. However, the restoration of grace in the life of Peter should remind us to seek the things which are above and learn to ignore the things which are on earth.

We are traveling on our journey toward eternity and whatever happens while we remain on earth is only temporary and should be treated in such a manner.

Aren't we careful to keep our jewelry stored in a safe while we treat an empty milk carton or a used jar of mayonnaise in an opposite fashion? One item is of lasting value, the others are temporary.

THE BIBLE: OUR ETERNAL ROCK

With eternity in view, the apostle Paul admonished us with the following words, *"For this corruptible must put on incorruption, and this mortal must put on immortality. So when this corruptible shall have put on incorruption, and this mortal shall have put on immortality, then shall be brought to pass the saying that is written, Death is swallowed up in victory. O death, where is thy sting? O grave, where is thy victory? The sting of death is sin; and the strength of sin is the law. But thanks be to God, which giveth us the victory through our Lord Jesus Christ. Therefore, my beloved brethren, be ye stedfast, unmoveable, always abounding in the work of the Lord, forasmuch as ye know that your labour is not in vain in the Lord"* (1st Corinthians 15:53-58).

THE BIBLE: A HISTORICAL BOOK

The Bible is the authority of the Christian church and an instruction manual for all believers. What is so remarkable about the Bible is that it can also be used as a historical document where we find names and locations of government officials such as kings and rulers, as well as the geographical extent of their kingdoms. The accuracy of history is documented by names, places, and dates.

For example, the book of Nehemiah begins with the words, *"The words of Nehemiah the son of Hachaliah. And it came to pass in the month Chisleu, in the twentieth year, as I was in Shushan the palace"* (verse 1). This could be argued because someone may not know what is referred to by the "twentieth year;" however, verse 2 offers an explanation, *"That Hanani, one of my brethren, came, he and certain men of Judah; and I asked them concerning the Jews that had escaped, which were left of the captivity, and concerning Jerusalem."* So we see that this took place in approximately 450 B.C., after the fall of Jerusalem when the Jews were living in captivity.

THE BIBLE: A SCIENTIFIC BOOK

The Bible is also a scientific book in that it precisely declares how the world began, *"In the beginning God created the heaven and the earth."* No credible scientist or study can disprove the statements of the Bible. Only recently have we discovered that the world is round and turns on its own axis suspended in space. That was no news for Job who lived approximately 3,500 years ago. He said, *"He stretcheth out the north over the empty place, and hangeth the earth upon nothing"* (Job 26:7).

In chapter 28:5 he says, *"As for the earth, out of it cometh bread: and under it is turned up as it were fire."* Very plainly this tells us that the earth brings forth food and deep in the earth, it is *"as it were fire."* That's no mystery today. Several miles into the center of the earth is unimaginable heat which sometimes comes to the surface through the eruption of volcanoes.

Do you want to know about politics? Read the Bible. Biology? It's in the Word of God. If we wish to know the secret of life, we will find it in the Scriptures. All of the philosophers in the world cannot attain the knowledge that's contained in the Bible. The Bible is an excellent textbook for studying history, geography, science and biology: seeking the truth, and exposing the lies.

THE BIBLE SAYS "COME"

The Bible speaks a lot about the future and reveals the mystery of life; past, present, and future.

I heard a theologian once say, "The Word of God can be summarized by one word, 'come'." How true. The Bible is God's invitation to man to come to Him. Man severed his relationship with God when he sinned. Consequently, the laws of God were violated and man was hopelessly lost in his sin. Because we could not atone for our own sin, God sent His Son Jesus to die on Calvary's cross, pouring out His life in His blood for the sins of mankind. Now, the invitation is, "come to Jesus and receive eternal life."

Our first parents lost eternal life by believing the lies of the devil. Today, man can regain it by believing that Jesus paid the penalty for our sin once and for all.

SIMPLE SALVATION

What is so amazing about the Bible is the simplicity of salvation. We don't have to climb the highest mountains to obtain knowledge, nor do we have to suffer immeasurably in order to be saved. In fact, we don't even have to work for many years until we have reached a qualifying stage for salvation. The Bible tells us that we may come to Jesus at any time, simply by believing that

Jesus is the Savior who purchased us from the powers of darkness and death, *"But as many as received him, to them gave he power to become the sons of God, even to them that believe on his name"* (John 1:12).

If its so simple, why does it seem so complicated? Because the enemy of our souls does not want us to be saved so he glorifies the things of the world to the point that nothing else seems important. However, God's intention is revealed in 1st Timothy 2:4, *"Who will have all men to be saved, and to come unto the knowledge of the truth."*

Believing in God means following the instruction of the Scripture. In reading the Bible, we find that the men and women of God who did great things were prayer warriors. However, prayer is not a one-way street. The Spirit of God guides us when we are born again. The object of prayer originates in the heart of God who puts it on our heart via the Holy Spirit. The Holy Spirit speaks to our spirit and we begin to pray, returning it to God. If the two-way communication is interrupted by sin, then we cannot expect an answer to our prayer.

For the sake of clarity, let us remember that God speaks to us through His Word, and we communicate with Him through prayer.

GUIDELINE TO WAR

I am afraid that many prayers in the Church today can be considered selfish. We are admonished to pray always and for all things, but that prayer is not detached from our personal life in Christ. Prayer is a spiritual weapon that cannot be used for carnal purposes. Under the inspiration of the Holy Spirit, Paul conveyed these instructions relating to our life in Christ, *"Finally, my brethren, be strong in the Lord, and in the power of his might. Put on the whole armour of God, that ye may be able to stand against the wiles of the devil. For we wrestle not against flesh and blood, but against principalities, against powers, against the rulers of the darkness of this world, against spiritual wickedness in high places. Wherefore take unto you the whole armour of God, that ye may be able to withstand in the evil day, and having done all, to stand. Stand therefore, having your loins girt about with truth, and having on the breastplate of righteousness; And your feet shod with the preparation of the gospel of peace; Above all, taking the shield of faith, wherewith ye shall be able to quench all the fiery darts of the wicked. And take the helmet of salvation, and the sword of the Spirit, which is the word of God: Praying always with all prayer and supplication in the Spirit, and watching thereunto with all perseverance and supplication for all saints"* (Ephesians 6:10-18). How often do we hear prayers like, "Lord, strengthen me" or "Give me more power?" These verses clearly say that we should be strong in the Lord, not in ourselves, and in the power of His might, not our might.

CHAPTER 6

MOSES: A Man Of God

"And when the LORD saw that he turned aside to see, God called unto him out of the midst of the bush, and said, Moses, Moses. And he said, Here am I. And he said, Draw not nigh hither: put off thy shoes from off thy feet, for the place whereon thou standest is holy ground"

Exodus 3:4-5

The Bible is filled with many other examples of men and women who's lives relate to the topic of our study, but we will now focus our attention on one of the most powerful and impressive figures in Israel's history: Moses. The second chapter of Exodus relates his birth, his escape from the certain death of Pharaoh, and his adoption by Pharaoh's daughter. When comparing the Exodus account to the seventh chapter of Acts, we can conclude that Moses was aware that he was a Hebrew, *"...Moses was learned in all the wisdom of the Egyptians, and was mighty in words and in deeds"* (Acts 7:22). History confirms that Egypt was the epitome of intellect at this time. Their advanced and refined civilization is validated by some of the mighty buildings throughout the land which have remained until this day.

For the first 40 years of his life, Moses lived in the house of Pharaoh, which we presume to have been a royal palace of splendor, glory, comfort, and riches.

Then Moses decided to visit his people, the Hebrews, *"And when he was full forty years old, it came into his heart to visit his brethren the children of Israel"* (Acts 7:23).

Moses' life was about to change. In exchange for the grandeur of the palace, he chose to tend sheep in the desert for his father-in-law Jethro.

What a dramatic change this must have been for him. Moses grew up with all the advantages of education, food, clothing, and shelter. Now he voluntarily chose to live in a tent and rely on the work of his hands.

MOSES MEETS GOD

Moses was tending the flock when he saw the burning bush, *"And the angel of the LORD appeared unto him in a flame of fire out of the midst of a bush: and he looked, and, behold, the bush burned with fire, and the bush was not consumed. And Moses said, I will now turn aside, and see this great sight, why the bush is not burnt"* (Exodus 3:2-3). We must assume that Moses, who had already spent so many years in Pharaoh's home, had probably forgotten about the God of Israel.

Moses did what any normal person would have done, he went over to inspect the bush and figure out why it was not burnt. It was at that time Moses met with God, *"And when the LORD saw that he turned aside to see, God called unto him out of the midst of the bush, and said, Moses, Moses. And he said, Here am I. And he said, Draw not nigh hither: put off thy shoes from off thy feet, for the place whereon thou standest is holy ground. Moreover he said, I am the God of thy father, the God of Abraham, the God of Isaac, and the God of Jacob. And Moses hid his face; for he was afraid to look upon God. And the LORD said, I have surely seen the affliction of my people which are in Egypt, and have heard their cry by reason of their taskmasters; for I know their sorrows; And I am come down to deliver them out of the hand of the Egyptians, and to bring them up out of that land unto a good land and a large, unto a land flowing with milk and honey; unto the place of the Canaanites, and the Hittites, and the Amorites, and the Perizzites, and the Hivites, and the Jebusites. Now therefore, behold, the cry of the children of Israel is come unto me: and I have also seen the oppression wherewith the Egyptians oppress them. Come now therefore, and I will send thee unto Pharaoh, that thou mayest bring forth my people the children of Israel out of Egypt"* (verses 4-10).

THE ETERNAL "I AM"

After God presented His case to him, Moses answered, *"...Who am I, that I should go unto Pharaoh, and that I should bring forth the children of Israel out of Egypt"* (verse 11). God reminded Moses, *"...I will be with thee..."* (verse 12). Moses was getting uncomfortable. He knew he was in the presence of God, but tried desperately to get out of this calling and prayed, *"Behold, when I come unto the children of Israel, and shall say unto them, The God of your fathers hath sent me unto you; and they shall say to me, What is his name? what shall I say unto them?"* (verse 13). What was God's response? *"...I AM THAT I AM..."* (verse 14).

I have read a number of explanations regarding the phrase, *"I AM THAT I AM."* I believe we need to simplify this matter and take these words for exactly what they say. Why didn't God say, "I am Jehovah, the creator of heaven and earth?" Because Moses was raised in the home of an Egyptian, so He knew that they served many different gods. Apparently Moses only understood the relationship of God and man by means of an idol. Of course he knew about the God of Abraham, Isaac, and Jacob, but at the same time, he also experienced the various idols he had been introduced to in the land of Egypt, particularly in the house of Pharaoh. In other words, Moses wanted to know which one of the god's He was? God was not about to be put on a list named among many other gods. He is the eternal, everlasting, omnipotent, omnipresent *"I AM!"* It was necessary for the Lord to give Moses a history lesson recalling the promises He made to Abraham, Isaac, and Jacob. Remember, He had already introduced Himself to Moses in verse 6 as *"...the God of thy father, the God of Abraham, the God of Isaac, and the God of Jacob...."* In verses 15 and 16 He repeated His identity in which Moses was to convey to the Israelites and the elders. Then the Lord gave Moses an abbreviated list of what He had already given to Abraham, Isaac, and Jacob, even identifying the original inhabitants of the Promised Land. God added the promise that they would be cast out and that Israel was destined to receive a land flowing with milk and honey.

THE ROD OF MOSES

Even after this startling revelation Moses was still not convinced, so he prayed again, *"...behold, they will not believe me, nor hearken unto my voice: for they will say, The LORD hath not appeared unto thee"* (Exodus 4:1). God responded in a simple manner in order to teach Moses that He was who He said He was. He asked, *"What is that in thine hand?"* (verse 2). Moses replied, *"A rod."* God instructed Moses to throw it on the ground and when he did, the rod became a serpent. God then told him to pick up the serpent, and when he did, it changed back into a rod. This was a visible miracle that helped Moses to believe.

THE LEPROUS HAND

Moses was justifiably concerned about confronting the elders and the children of Israel with God's proclamation and promise to lead them out of Egypt. Fearing that they would question and reject him, he brought his petition to the Lord. As a result, the Lord performed a number of miracles designed to cure the Israelites of their unbelief. After changing Moses' rod into a serpent, God instructed Moses to put his hand into his bosom. When Moses took his hand out, it was leprous. Then God said, *"Put thine hand into thy bosom again. And he put his hand into his bosom again; and plucked it out of his bosom, and, behold, it was turned again as his other flesh"* (Exodus 4:7). Now Moses had two very important signs to present to the elders of Israel that would confirm he was in fact sent by the God of Abraham, Isaac, and Jacob. The Lord considered the fact that Israel would not believe, *"...if they will not believe thee, neither hearken to the voice of the first sign, that they will believe the voice of the latter sign"* (Exodus 4:8). The Bible does not record Moses' reaction to the second sign, both of which God referred to as a voice, meaning that it was a visible sign from the Lord.

WATER BECOMES BLOOD

God continued, *"...it shall come to pass, if they will not believe also these two signs, neither hearken unto thy voice, that thou shalt take of the water of the river, and pour it upon the dry land: and the water which thou takest out of the river shall become blood upon the dry land"* (verse 9). In the event the elders and the Israelites challenged the fact that Moses was sent by God, he was now equipped with a series of signs that would validate his proclamation.

One would think that after all of these direct instructions from the Lord, Moses would say, "Yes Lord, here I am, send me." Instead, Moses prayed again, *"...O my Lord, I am not eloquent, neither heretofore, nor since thou hast spoken unto thy servant: but I am slow of speech, and of a slow tongue"* (verse 10). Even after God declared that He was the One who *"...hath made man's mouth"* and *"...maketh the dumb, or deaf, or the seeing, or the blind,"* Moses was still not convinced. He prayed, *"O my Lord, send, I pray thee, by the hand of him whom thou wilt send"* (verse 13). This is an example of stubborn unbelief. The Lord had just ordained Moses for this important task that would bring his people out of bondage! Moses should have been overjoyed; instead, we read that he prayed to the Lord to send someone else.

Understandably, the Lord grew impatient, *"And the anger of the LORD was kindled against Moses, and he said, Is not Aaron the Levite thy brother? I know that he can speak well. And also, behold, he cometh forth to meet thee: and when he seeth thee, he will be glad in his heart. And thou shalt speak unto him, and put words in his mouth: and I will be with thy mouth, and with his mouth, and will teach you what ye shall do. And he shall be thy spokesman unto the people: and he shall be, even he shall be to thee instead of a mouth, and thou shalt be to him instead of God"* (verses 14-16).

Eventually Moses obliged and became the great leader of the Israelites, bringing the Hebrews out of slavery and into the liberty of God's rulership.

MOSES BELIEVES GOD

A remarkable event occurred when the liberated Israelites saw the Egyptians for the last time, *"And when Pharaoh drew nigh, the children of Israel lifted up their eyes, and, behold, the Egyptians marched after them; and they were sore afraid: and the children of Israel cried out unto the LORD"* (Exodus 14:10). Once again, the Israelites believed only what they saw, and what they saw were the Egyptian troops marching after them. The Israelites rebelled as a result of their unbelief from the very beginning. They had already experienced the mighty miracles Moses performed before Pharaoh; they saw and heard the cries of all the Egyptian families who lost their firstborn while Israel received total protection; yet, they hardened their hearts and rebelled against the Word of God.

Moses answered them, *"...Fear ye not, stand still, and see the salvation of the LORD, which he will shew to you to day: for the Egyptians whom ye have seen to day, ye shall see them again no more for ever"* (verse 13). What a courageous statement! Why? The answer is found in verse 14, *"The LORD shall fight for you, and ye shall hold your peace."*

MOSES RESPONSIBLE FOR ISRAEL

Immediately following Moses' statement we read of something rather strange. It almost seems as if some words were left out because verse 15 reads, *"And the LORD said unto Moses, Wherefore criest thou unto me? speak unto the children of Israel, that they go forward."* We already read in verse 10 that, *"...the children of Israel cried out unto the LORD,"* but there is no indication that Moses prayed in this situation. As a matter of fact, Moses was totally convinced that God would do that which He had promised; yet, the Lord opposed Moses, *"Wherefore criest thou unto me?"* I believe the hidden mystery lies in the fact that God had ordained Moses as the leader of the Israelites; therefore, Moses was responsible for what the people did.

Finally, Israel moved through the water as if they were on dry ground. The water separated to the left and right, and when the Egyptians tried to take advantage of this miraculous occurrence, their mighty armies drowned.

In spite of the fact that Israel was a chosen nation that experienced so many miracles and confirmations that the God of Israel was the God of heaven and earth, they continued to rebel against the Word of God.

ISRAEL'S UNBELIEF

The tragedy of Israel's unbelief is later recorded by the apostle Paul in 1st Corinthians 10:1-10, *"Moreover, brethren, I would not that ye should be ignorant, how that all our fathers were under the cloud, and all passed through the sea; And were all baptized unto Moses in the cloud and in the sea; And did all eat the same spiritual meat; And did all drink the same spiritual drink: for they drank of that spiritual Rock that followed them: and that Rock was Christ. But with many of them God was not well pleased: for they were overthrown in the wilderness. Now these things were our examples, to the intent we should not lust after evil things, as they also lusted. Neither be ye idolaters, as were some of them; as it is written, The people sat down to eat and drink, and rose up to play. Neither let us commit fornication, as some of them committed, and fell in one day three and twenty thousand. Neither let us tempt Christ, as some of them also tempted, and were destroyed of serpents. Neither murmur ye, as some of them also murmured, and were destroyed of the destroyer"* (verse 1-10). It is extremely important that we take the events that transpired in, with, and through the nation of Israel to heart because they are an example for us.

MOSES' DIALOGUE FOR ISRAEL

After everything the Israelites had seen taking place since they were led out of Egypt by the Lord, the most obscene betrayal took place while Moses remained in the presence of the Lord for 40 days and 40 nights. The children of Israel forsook the God whom they vowed to serve and replaced Him with an inanimate golden calf! The close union God considered Moses to have with His people is evident from Exodus 32:7, *"And the LORD said unto Moses, Go, get thee down; for thy people, which thou broughtest out of the land of Egypt, have corrupted themselves."* Notice how God refers to the Israelites as *"thy people."* No longer does He say that it was He who brought them out of the land of Egypt, but *"which **thou** broughtest* *out of the land of Egypt."* God separated Himself from His people and His work of salvation after Israel sinned by making themselves a golden calf and said, *"...These be thy gods, O Israel, which have brought thee up out of the land of Egypt"* (Exodus 32:8).

Now we see quite a different Moses. He had completely changed from the one who refused to obey God's commands to actually identifying himself with the sins of his own people, although in this matter he was innocent. Moses' position had changed; he was no longer a representative of God to the people, but a representative of the people to God assuming the office of priest.

MOSES DEFENDS GOD'S HONOR

Moses pleaded with God for his people, *"And Moses besought the LORD his God, and said, LORD, why doth thy wrath wax hot against thy people, which thou hast brought forth out of the land of Egypt with great power, and with a mighty hand?"* (Exodus 32:11). Moses was standing on the promises of God. He did not accept that the people were his people or that he was the one who led them out of Egypt.

Moses went even further to defend God's honor, *"Wherefore should the Egyptians speak, and say, For mischief did he bring them out, to slay them in the mountains, and to consume them from the face of the earth? Turn from thy fierce wrath, and repent of this evil against thy people"* (verse 12). These were not empty words, they were a matter of life and death, more importantly, eternal life and death. It is obvious that Moses was very close to his people as illustrated by his standing between the wrath of God and the sin of Israel. This is so dramatically expressed in verse 32, *"Yet now, if thou wilt forgive their sin–; and if not, blot me, I pray thee, out of thy book which thou hast written."* God replied, *"...Whosoever hath sinned against me, him will I blot out of my book. Therefore now go, lead the people unto the place of which I have spoken unto thee: behold, mine Angel shall go before thee: nevertheless in the day when I visit, I will visit their sin upon them"* (verse 33–34).

MOSES SEEKS GOD'S PRESENCE

Although Moses received an answer to his prayer to forgive the sin of his people, he realized the difference in God's promises. The Lord did not say, "I will be with thee" or "I will go before thee" but very specifically, *"mine Angel shall go before thee."* Moses was not satisfied with this compromise. God's original promise was that He would be with them so he pleaded with God in Exodus 33:13, *"Now therefore, I pray thee, if I have found grace in thy sight, shew me now thy way, that I may know thee, that I may find grace in thy sight: and consider that this nation is thy people."* God's response to Moses' plea was, *"My presence shall go with thee, and I will give thee rest"* (verse 14).

GOD'S GLORY AND MOSES

An amazing thing happened in the relationship between the Lord and Moses, *"And the LORD said unto*

Moses, I will do this thing also that thou hast spoken: for thou hast found grace in my sight, and I know thee by name" (verse 17). Then, another unanswered prayer followed, Moses said, *"I beseech thee, shew me thy glory"* (verse 18).

If the Lord had responded to Moses' prayer, he would have died instantaneously, *"...Thou canst not see my face: for there shall no man see me, and live"* (verse 20). Then the most glorious event in Moses' life is revealed, *"And the LORD said, Behold, there is a place by me, and thou shalt stand upon a rock: And it shall come to pass, while my glory passeth by, that I will put thee in a clift of the rock, and will cover thee with my hand while I pass by: And I will take away mine hand, and thou shalt see my back parts: but my face shall not be seen"* (verses 21-23). Who was this Rock? The Lord Jesus Christ who is a cleft for us: "Rock of Ages, cleft for me, let me hide myself in thee, let the water and the blood, from thy wounded side which flowed, be of sin the double cure, save from wrath and make me pure."

Dear friend, in closing, let us not wish for the Lord to reveal Himself to us in a miraculous way. Why do I say that? Because the more we experience and see with our eyes of flesh, the less capable we will be of believing. Jesus said, *"Blessed are they that see not and believe."* We have the Bible which is God's full counsel to man. The answer to all of our questions are found there. The more we occupy ourselves with the precious Word of God, the more we will recognize the glory of Him who promised, *"Lo, I am with you always, even unto the end of the world."*

CHAPTER 7

JOB:
Patient In Tribulation

"...the LORD gave and the LORD hath taken away; blessed
be the name of the LORD"

Job 1:21

Whentthen we consider those who have suffered great loss, the first person who should come to our mind is Job. This great man of God was wealthy in material possessions, but everything–including his family, livelihood and even his health–was taken from him. Before we begin our study of this biblical character, let's first set the scene for one of the greatest circumstances of calamity and tragedy to ever befall a person in the history of humanity. What we learn from Job in this chapter will give us a deeper understanding of why God chooses to answer some prayers and not others; of the fact that His will is perfect; of the precept that He only does that which is for His glory and our good; and of how unanswered prayer teaches us perseverance, which builds character. Throughout the course of this horrible ordeal, instead of becoming bitter and angry with God, Job came to know the Lord personally so that in the end he would say, *"I have heard of thee by the hearing of the ear: but now mine eye seeth thee"* (Job 42:5). Instead of asking God why He allows us to suffer, we must learn to ask Him what He wants to teach us through our suffering. As difficult as it may sometimes be, our response should be, "If it brings You glory, Lord, I will bear this burden without complaining."

INTERCESSION IN VAIN?

Job, who may have been a contemporary of Terah, Abraham's father, lived in a land called Uz, which was where the testing of his faith took place. Job had ten children who, even when they were grown, would gather for family parties that would last several days. This indicates how Job raised his children. Whenever they had a feast, Job interceded on their behalf. Were his burnt offerings and prayers in vain? When he later stood before the caskets of his dead children, he didn't ask, "God, how could You allow this to happen?" Instead, he gave God the glory and said, "...*the LORD gave, and the LORD hath taken away; blessed be the name of the LORD*" (Job 1:21).

"DOST THOU STILL RETAIN THINE INTEGRITY?"

It is ironic that the enemy took Job's children and all he owned, yet spared his wife. I believe that it is safe to assume that Job's wife remained because Satan wanted to use her against him, just as he had once used Eve to deceive Adam. It is rather difficult to imagine that on top of all that he had just gone through, the mother of his ten children dangled temptation in front of him. Pitifully, Job sat among the ashes scraping himself with a piece of broken pottery. Job's wife must have wondered, "What has your godliness brought you? Only painful losses, broken pieces and ashes." Her advice to Job was, "...*curse God, and die.*" At this point, you would think that Job would have found a glimmer of attraction in this idea as a possible way to end his suffering, but this faithful giant did not waver. Anyone else would have gladly dropped dead rather than endure the physical, mental and emotional torture he had experienced.

I believe that because the devil challenged the basis of Job's faith, God gave Job the grace he needed to prove to the devil that his faith in God was not based on his wealth.

Recently a house in our neighborhood burned down. The owners, just back from vacation, stood among the ruins to survey their loss. Everything that they had worked hard for had been destroyed in a matter of minutes. This caused me to reflect on Job's trials. Had we been in a similar situation and lost everything, how would that affect our faith or view of God?

If we had the opportunity to ask the martyrs who were burned at the stake, killed by wild beasts in the Roman arena or tortured to death, "Do you still hold on to your integrity?" How do you think they would have answered? One martyr in particular responded to the Roman official responsible for his condemnation in the following way, "How can I renounce my wonderful Lord whom I have served all my life, even in my old age?" Similarly, with the apostle Paul, they confessed that they wanted, *"...to depart, and to be with Christ; which is far better"* (Philippians 1:23).

A COMPASSIONATE START

When the news of Job's severe misfortune reached his friends, they decided it would be best to come alongside of him in his time of need. This gesture began with good intentions, they were very concerned about Job's well-being and were saddened by this unexpected turn of events, *"And when they lifted up their eyes afar off, and knew him not, they lifted up their voice, and wept; and they rent every one his mantle, and sprinkled dust upon their heads toward heaven. So they sat down with him upon the ground seven days and seven nights, and none spake a word unto him: for they saw that his grief was very great"* (Job 2:12-13). So it's plain to see that Job's friends were genuinely concerned. Putting aside their responsibilities and obligations, they chose to sit on the ground with him in silence for seven days.

ACCUSATIONS - THE WRONG CONTINUATION

Unfortunately, this show of kindness was short-lived. In response to Job's lamentation over his suffering, his friends used the opportunity to present their own conclusions and opinions. We find very profound truths in their speeches, but they spoke these truths in the wrong context. Not everything that they said was wrong, but the summary of their counsel was that it was necessary for Job to suffer this judgment because there must have been sin hidden somewhere in his life. As the conversation went on, their motives turned ugly until Job finally answered them, *"I have heard many such things: miserable comforters are ye all. Shall vain words have an end? or what emboldeneth thee that thou answerest?"* (Job 16:2-3).

WHAT DID GOD THINK OF JOB'S FRIENDS?

In the end the tables were turned; the accused was acquitted by God Himself, while his accusers now stood guilty, *"And it was so, that after the LORD had spoken these words unto Job, the LORD said to Eliphaz the Temanite, My wrath is kindled against thee, and against thy two friends: for ye have not spoken of me the thing that is right, as my servant Job hath"* (Job 42:7) What did Job's friends think of their counsel? More importantly, what did the Lord think of it? Job's response to the accusations of his *"miserable comforters"* was more acceptable to God than their hypocritical speeches.

JOB JUSTIFIED

Job's "friends" had to humbly accept and admit that God was right, and then they had to approach Job so that he would intercede for them. They were instructed to *"...take unto you now seven bullocks and seven rams, and go to my servant Job, and offer up for yourselves a burnt offering; and my servant Job shall pray for you: for him will I accept: lest I deal with you after your folly, in that ye have not spoken of me the thing which is right, like my servant Job"* (Job 42:8).

The pride Job's friends must have felt when they were "counselling" him had surely faded by now. The trio had to approach God with their deflated ego, *"So Eliphaz the Temanite and Bildad the Shuhite and Zophar the Naamathite went, and did according as the LORD commanded them: the LORD also accepted Job"* (verse 9). From this situation we see that giving comfort is an art. The apostle Paul pointed to our source of comfort when he testified, *"Blessed be God, even the Father of our Lord Jesus Christ, the Father of mercies, and the God of all comfort; Who comforteth us in all our tribulation, that we may be able to comfort them which are in any trouble, by the comfort wherewith we ourselves are comforted of God"* (2nd Corinthians 1:3-4). Because Job experienced the God of all comfort, he could help his friends. When we are comforted by God, we can comfort others.

DOES PRAYER CHANGE GOD'S MIND?

The prophet Ezekiel mentions Job as a man who was righteous before God. At that time Jerusalem was so ripe for judgment that not even the intercession of Job, Noah or Daniel could deter their impending doom, *"Though these three men, Noah, Daniel, and Job, were in it, they should deliver but their own souls by their righteousness, saith the Lord GOD...Though Noah, Daniel, and Job, were in it, as I live, saith the Lord GOD, they shall deliver neither son nor daughter; they shall but deliver their own souls by their righteousness"* (Ezekiel 14:14 and 20). These three men can be considered a type of savior in a sense that Noah saved his family (Hebrews 11:7), Daniel saved the wise men in Babylon from execution (Daniel 2:12, 16, 18 and 24), and Job saved his friends from severe punishment through his intercession (Job 42:8).

NOT AGAINST FLESH AND BLOOD

The book of Job clearly illustrates that Satan, a murderer from the beginning, had to have help to accomplish God's plan in world history and in the lives of individual Christians. This book teaches us that the enemy has access to the throne of God, but can only act with the Lord's permission. Satan's ultimate goal is always destruction, which is contrary to God's intention to bless by teaching and leading us into a deeper knowledge and fellowship with Him. God used the enemy to take away everything dear to Job's heart. Only in this way could Job receive even greater blessings.

But God went even further, *"Then the LORD answered Job out of the whirlwind, and said, Who is this that darkeneth counsel by words without knowledge?"* (Job 38:1-2). By so doing, the Lord convicted his servant regarding his limited knowledge of God and creation, as well as the traditional godliness which he was very proud of, so that Job was deeply affected by the words of the Creator to the point that he confessed, *"Wherefore I abhor myself, and repent in dust and ashes"* (Job 42:6).

The Lord predestined the beginning and end of Job's suffering. Job could rightly have said, "Dear God, thank You for not answering my prayers." God had even greater blessings in store for His servant, *"...the LORD gave Job twice as much as he had before...the LORD blessed the latter end of Job more than his beginning..."* (Job 42:10 and 12). James referred to this when he wrote, *"Ye have heard of the patience of Job, and have seen the end of the Lord; that the Lord is very pitiful, and of tender mercy"* (James 5:11).

For the Christian, there are two completely different causes for Satan's attacks. First, Satan attacks only with God's permission to test a person's faith and obedience;

and second, he attacks when a person deliberately and willfully clings to sin which demands God's discipline (the sin unto death). In the first case, the believer honors God through patient suffering; in the second, the Christian living in sin disgraces his Lord and consequently experiences his chastening judgment. Let us remind ourselves daily of the promise, *"Blessed is the man that endureth temptation: for when he is tried, he shall receive the crown of life, which the Lord hath promised to them that love him"* (James 1:12).

CHAPTER 8

JONAH:
Compassion Or Judgment?

*"Now the word of the LORD came unto Jonah the son of
Amittai, saying, Arise, go to Ninevah, that great city, and
cry against it; for their wickedness is come up before me"*

Jonah 1:1-2

TWO VASTLY DIFFERENT PRAYERS

We'll now shift our focus to Jonah, another man who became the subject of a dramatic scenario which God used to reveal his power and mercy. The book of Jonah offers a glimpse into this man's life, actions and human emotions with an amazing openness that reveals two vastly different reactions in prayer to God's actions.

Jonah was from southern Galilee and was chosen by God to bring a special message of repentance to the Assyrians living in Ninevah. Located east of the Tigris River, Ninevah was the residence of the Assyrian kings. For various reasons Jonah didn't want to be that messenger, so he headed for Tarshish, disobeying God's clear command.

But let's not jump to conclusions or judge Jonah too hastily. Remember how the Lord had to speak to Peter twice until he would enter into the house of Cornelius, the Roman centurion, and open the door of faith to the Gentiles? Contempt for the godless Gentiles was deeply rooted in the heart of all godly Jews–they did not want to contaminate themselves through contact with them. We must keep this in mind when looking into Jonah's life because undoubtedly, Jonah's patriotism must have played a part in his resistance to God's command. As we track this unwilling servant's prayer life throughout this drama, we see a man responding to God's actions with prayers of both praise and anger.

1. Praise Out of the Depths of the Sea

The Lord resorted to an unusual means to set Jonah

straight. The bizarre event–allowing Jonah to be swallowed by a fish–may seem unbelievable, but Jesus confirmed this historical event when He referred to the three days and three nights Jonah spent in the belly of the fish as He was speaking to the Jews at Nazareth so that they would believe on Him through this Messianic sign of His resurrection (Matthew 12:40).

Can you imagine what it must have been like for Jonah to be swallowed by a fish? *"Then Jonah prayed unto the LORD his God out of the fish's belly, And said, I cried by reason of mine affliction unto the LORD, and he heard me; out of the belly of hell cried I, and thou heardest my voice"* (Jonah 2:1-2). The Lord always hears when His children cry to Him in extreme distress.

Can you possibly fall any deeper than the depths of the sea? Jonah's first reaction to his circumstances must have been one of hopelessness as he faced what seemed like certain death, *"I went down to the bottoms of the mountains; the earth with her bars was about me for ever."* But then he rejoiced over his salvation: *"...yet hast thou brought up my life from corruption, O LORD my God"* (Jonah 2:6). Jonah was in complete desperation, yet he knew who he could turn to, *"When my soul fainted within me I remembered the LORD: and my prayer came in unto thee, into thine holy temple"* (verse 7). Jonah did not cry to a lifeless, heathen idol, but to the living, eternal God of heaven. Despite his dark prison he was able to rejoice, *"...I will sacrifice unto thee with the voice of thanksgiving; I will pay that I have vowed. Salvation is of the LORD"* (verse 9). Not surprisingly, God's method of punishment allowed Jonah to see his disobedience, and sent him on his way to warn the Assyrians that judgment was upon them. However, although Jonah was physically heading in the right direction, his attitude toward the Assyrians was spiritually–and sinfully–wrong.

2. Self-Realization or World Mission?

Jonah, who had just emerged from a desperate situation having learned a powerful lesson was about to be taught another. His complete disregard for the 120,000 souls of Ninevah was shameful. I believe that is the reason why God allowed the Assyrians to take Jonah's message to heart and repent. Jonah should have rejoiced that God gave him a successful trip, and he should have been equally ashamed by his attitude for these people. But instead, Jonah got angry, *"And he prayed unto the LORD, and said, I pray thee, O LORD, was not this my saying, when I was yet in my country? Therefore I fled before unto Tarshish: for I knew that thou art a gracious God, and merciful, slow to anger, and of great kindness, and repentest thee of the evil. Therefore now, O LORD, take, I beseech thee, my life from me; for it is better for me to die than to live"* (Jonah 4:2-3). Jonah tried to justify his actions by telling God that he knew that He was merciful and would not pour out His wrath on Ninevah, so there really was no need for him to go to the Assyrians in the first place.

ISRAEL, THE ELDER SON

Doesn't this remind us of the older son's attitude in the

account of the prodigal son? His good-for-nothing younger brother had come home after squandering his inheritance yet his father rejoiced and made a feast in his honor, *"And he was angry, and would not go in: therefore came his father out, and intreated him"* (Luke 15:28), indeed serves as a picture of Israel, who despised the Gentiles (the younger brother) because they were far from God and lost in idolatry and immortality. How great is the Father's love for the younger son as it is for the older brother, so that both can enter into the full enjoyment of the Father's house!

"DOEST THOU WELL?"

The Lord wanted His discontent servant to think the matter over as He asked, *"...Doest thou well to be angry?"* (Jonah 4:4). But Jonah did not answer Him and ran away like a stubborn child who didn't get his way.

To the east of the city Jonah found himself a place to build a booth from which he could watch what happened to the great city. How patient was God with the angry prophet? In another attempt to liberate the prophet from his resentment the Lord caused a castor oil plant to grow overnight. *"Jonah was exceeding glad of the gourd,"* because it gave him shade so that he could cool down a little, but what he didn't see was God's intention for providing the plant in the first place!

THE PARADOXICAL PRAYER OF A MAN WHO IS TIRED OF LIFE

Initially God used a large fish to change Jonah's attitude. Now He uses a little worm, *"...and it smote the gourd that it withered. And it came to pass, when the sun did arise, that God prepared a vehement east wind; and the sun beat upon the head of Jonah, that he fainted..."* (Jonah 4:7-8). God did all of this to bring His selfish servant to reason. The sun, together with a hot east wind sent by the Lord, brought a desperately unhappy Jonah to this disturbing realization: he wanted to die. Once again the Lord asked him, *"Doest thou well to be angry, even unto death?"* Jonah replied, *"I do well to be angry, even unto death."* For many, humiliation can bring us to this point. Jonah's national/Jewish patriotism, coupled with his unbroken self-confidence, made him tired of life and even sparked an anger with God over a plant that grew and withered in one night. Jonah still failed to see beyond the physical element of this plant until the Lord explained it to him.

THE CONVINCING COMPARISON

The Lord convicted Jonah of his bad attitude by saying to him, *"...Thou hast had pity on the gourd, for the which thou hast not laboured...And should not I spare Nineveh, that great city...?"* (verses 10 and 11). What significance did this one plant have in comparison to the people of Nineveh? Why was Jonah lamenting over a plant? The Lord wanted Jonah to understand His heartfelt compassion for these 120,000 people who *"...cannot discern between their right hand and their left hand."* These were people over which the clouds of judgment were gathering, and whom the Lord wanted to give another chance. The Lord always has the last word. We do not know how Jonah answered, but it is safe to assume that he thanked the Lord for choosing not to answer his request to die.

The book of Jonah ends rather abruptly and does not give any further information regarding the future of his ministry. Nevertheless, this account offers us another example of God not answering certain prayers for our good, and which will ultimately bring Him the most glory.

CHAPTER 9

ELIJAH: Zealous For God And Israel

"And it came to pass, as they still went on and talked, that behold, there appeared a chariot of fire, and horses of fire, and parted them both asunder; and Elijah went up by a whirlwind into heaven"

2nd Kings 2:11

One of the greatest prophets mentioned in Scripture is Elijah. Despite his greatness in challenging and confronting idolatry, Elijah also spoke a humble request to the Lord amidst much despair. Did God answer Elijah's prayer? Let's take a closer look into this prominent biblical character.

Elijah was from Gilead where his ministry focused on the northern kingdom. Elijah's ministry took place under the reigns of Ahab and Ahazaiah. When reading the ministerial account of Elijah, there can be no denying Elijah's zeal or success in eradicating pagan idol worship; however, with this spiritual high came a great despondency.

Elijah experienced glorious answer to prayer: a miraculous, unending supply of flour and oil; the revival of a dead boy; fire from heaven on Mt. Carmel that consumed the sacrifice; fire that also fell from heaven and killed his persecutors, and on top of all that, he was taken to heaven by God without tasting death! What a testimony!

On the other hand, Elijah also fell into extreme depression and lost his will to live, leading him to cry out to God to take him home. Again, as in the account of Jonah, the Lord did not answer this prayer. In Elijah's case, perhaps it was because He had further tasks in store for His servant.

ELIJAH VS. AHAB - GOD OR BAAL?

The prophecy about the dividing of the kingdom of

David and Solomon had been fulfilled. Under Solomon's son Rehoboam, the ten tribes had already separated from the house of David under the leadership of Jeroboam. Subsequently, there was a ten-tribe kingdom of Israel and the kingdom of Judah. While the northern kingdom had kings from various tribes and houses, Jerusalem, the capital of the southern kingdom only allowed descendants of David to sit on the throne.

Ahab was a godless king who, "...*did evil in the sight of the LORD above all that were before him*" (1st Kings 16:30). Against God's expressed will, Ahab married Jezebel, the daughter of the king of the Sidonians. Jezebel contributed in leading Ahab and all of Israel to worship Baal. Ahab even went so far as to have a temple built for Baal in Samaria.

Israel had been launched into a downward spiral since the reign of their first king, Jeroboam, and continued to decline under the rulership of his successors. In addition to Jeroboam's sin of making golden calves for the people to worship in Bethel and Dan so that they would have no need to travel to Jerusalem, now came Jezebel's worship of Baal with 800 priests! But Elijah entered the scene and stood before Ahab with this message of judgment from his heavenly government, "...*As the LORD God of Israel liveth, before whom I stand, there shall not be dew nor rain these years, but according to my word*" (1st Kings 17:1). This had been written in Deuteronomy 28:23-24, where Moses had laid the choice of blessing or curse before the people. Elijah stood before God, that is, he served the Most High, and he knew these words of judgment which the Lord confirmed in the heart of His prophet for this terrible time. Therefore, he boldly addressed Ahab in his palace because, like Abraham, Elijah was *"...fully persuaded that, what he (God) had promised, he was able also to perform"* (Romans 4:21).

POWER IN PRAYER

We can learn a great deal from Elijah. The content of James' letter points to the fact that God always hears the prayers of His children when they are based on His expressed promises in the Bible, and when they seek His glory, *"Elias was a man subject to like passions as we are, and he prayed earnestly that it might not rain: and it rained not on the earth by the space of three years and six months. And he prayed again, and the heaven gave rain, and the earth brought forth her fruit"* (James 5:17-18). The Baal worshippers believed that their god was the god of rain, which is why the drought God sent demonstrated His sovereign rule compared with the futility and accursed nature of the worship of Baal. Therefore, the drought struck the very heart of the Baal cult in Israel.

ANSWER FROM HEAVEN

A meeting of the priests of Baal and Elijah took place on Mount Carmel. The impotence of Baal worship was publicly exposed because no fire had fallen down on the sacrifice although the priests had cried out to Baal for hours. Elijah rebuilt the broken altar of the Lord at the time of the evening sacrifice, and the Lord confirmed His claim on Israel by letting fire fall from heaven consuming the sacrifice and even the water. *"And when all the people saw it, they fell on their faces: and they said, The LORD, he is the God; the LORD, he is the God"* (I Kings 18:39). The people were convinced. They had seen the fire with their own eyes. But would this cause them to believe and obey the Word of the Lord by removing all the idols from their lives and serving God alone? Emotional decisions are superficial and quickly lose significance. However, the two-edged sword of the Word pierces the heart and produces abiding fruit. Paul knew his people and wrote, *"For the Jews require a sign..."* (I Corinthians 1:22). When we look for signs and wonders and all types of manifestations, simple faith in the Word of God is soon forgotten.

THE ALTAR OF THE WHOLE PEOPLE

The Word of God says that Elijah, *"...took twelve stones according to the number of the tribes of the sons of Jacob...And with the stones he built an altar in the name of the LORD"* (I Kings 18:31-32). The prophet's task was limited to the northern kingdom. He did not build the altar of the Lord according to the number of the ten tribes, but according to the entire people of God. This is extremely significant because Israel consists of 12 tribes not 10.

In today's church, a leader must have a broad vision encompassing the entire kingdom of God. Those whose horizon is limited in the work entrusted them are not qualified to lead in the kingdom of God. God does not want to lead His kingdom according to the measure of a distorted number, or through the limitations of a part of the Body of Christ. Even if we must limit ourselves to only a part of the worldwide vineyard of God in our work, and even if we have to witness the division of God's people, we must cling in faith to the unity of God's people as a whole.

GOD DOES NOT LET GO OF HIS SERVANT

Two key people made the wrong decision after the impressive revelation of God on Mount Carmel: Jezebel, the demon queen, and Elijah, the prophet of God. Thoughts of revenge and murder arose in Jezebel's heart; she did not take advantage of the chance God gave her to make an about-face, but closed her ears to His mighty voice. Elijah also made a mistake because he did not remain standing before the Lord after his wonderful experience, which is why doubt and despondency got the upper hand in his heart.

THE UNANSWERED PRAYER CRY

What did Elijah do? *"But he himself went a day's journey into the wilderness, and came and sat down under a juniper tree: and he requested for himself that he might die; and said, It is enough; now, O LORD, take away my life; for I am not better than my fathers"* (1st King 19:4). Here we see that the God-inspired writer of this Scripture account does not engage in hero worship. On the contrary, this passage reveals people as God sees them. Elijah was at the end of his rope. This bold man was now gripped with fear and fled for his life, running through the kingdom of Judah to Beersheba, the southernmost city in the Negev. He left his servant behind and ran another whole day (about 24 kilometers or 15 miles) in the desert, threw himself under a shady juniper tree and prayed, *"It is enough; now, O LORD, take away my life..."*

The bold prophet is hardly recognizable as his attitude took a cowardly turn. He wanted to die because he was looking at his own self, his failure to withstand Jezebel and the circumstances that surrounded him. Like previous prophets, he was not able to fully eradicate the worship of Baal or bring about a widespread reformation of his people. This reality discouraged him.

Naturally after his long flight he was physically exhausted, which is probably one of the reasons he slept under the juniper tree, but it was his inner weariness that led to severe depression. Elijah literally lost sight of God. It had not been too long before when Elijah had told the widow in Zarephath who was faced with starvation to *"Fear not."* The mighty revelation of God on Mount Carmel was all but forgotten. Now, all he could see was the raging queen Jezebel.

Our spiritual condition is vastly affected by the direction of our eyes. There is a saying which goes, "Look at others and you will be disappointed, look at yourself and you will be discouraged; but looking to the Lord will renew your strength." Who among us has never experienced a period of complete discouragement?

Brothers and sisters, we must remember that we are redeemed from the slavery of negative feelings, *"Forasmuch as ye know that ye were not redeemed with corruptible things, as silver and gold, from your vain conversation received by tradition from your fathers; But with the precious blood of Christ, as of a lamb without blemish and without spot"* (1st Peter 1:18-19).

WHOLE HELP

What a beautiful picture it is to see the way in which the Lord helped His servant get back on his feet. First He took care of his basic human needs (later He would take care of his soul). A hungry, tired man must first eat and sleep, *"...then an angel touched him, and said unto him, Arise and eat."* A messenger from the Lord woke him and brought him food and drink, but did not reproach him. He spoke only these three words, and then he let him sleep again. True, heavenly help in the desert! *"And he looked, and, behold, there was a cake baken on the coals, and a cruse of water at his head. And he did eat and drink, and laid him down again."* We shouldn't say, "I would like to go to sleep and never wake up again!" Instead, we must eat, rest, go on vacation, learn to sleep enough again, and wake up refreshed every morning. Then we will see things with new eyes. God respects the laws of creation where His priests are concerned. Remember the words of this classic hymn:

156

"In the shadow of His wings,
There is rest, sweet rest;
There is rest from care and labor,
There is rest for friend and neighbor:
In the shadow of His wings, there is rest."

Despondency is an ingratitude for God's leading. Each day we should say the words of David, *"Bless the LORD, O my soul, and forget not all his benefits: Who forgiveth all thine iniquities; who healeth all thy diseases; Who redeemeth thy life from destruction; who crowneth thee with lovingkindness and tender mercies"* (Psalm 103:2-4).

This same Elijah was later taken to heaven in a chariot of fire in a whirlwind. That is our living hope, the taking home of the bride, *"...to be with the Lord for ever."*

NEW STEPS

What compassion God had on His tired servant! He let Elijah sleep again after eating, and only then comes the second stage of restoration, *"And the angel of the LORD came again the second time, and touched him, and said, Arise and eat; because the journey is too great for thee"* (1st Kings 19:7). Can't we take great comfort in the way God spoke to a man who wanted to die? His incomparable wisdom is clearly revealed in this act.

Today, this applies to a host of mentally-oppressed and depressed people who grow bitter in their self-pity. It is best to give people who are tired of living a new task which claims all of their attention. There are enough tasks. Hard work makes anyone feel appreciated and leaves no time to wallow in despondence.

Apparently, the journey did Elijah a great deal of good. It is the same way in which his people wandered centuries before under the leadership of Moses. Perhaps he murmured, "I am no better than my fathers. I failed...." However, it was on Mount Horeb, the mountain of God, where the Lord helped him see straight.

OVERCOME BY GOD

The prophet heard the Word of God again, *"...What doest thou here, Elijah?"* (1st Kings 19:9). In other words, "Elijah, you are no longer at your post in Israel. The seven thousand need leadership. What are you doing under a juniper tree?" How did Elijah answer Him? He did not say, "I fled, I have sinned..." but, *"...I have been very jealous for the LORD God of hosts: for the children of Israel have forsaken thy covenant...and I, even I only, am left; and they seek my life, to take it away"* (1st Kings 19:10). Elijah passed the blame to the Israelites and tried to make it seem as though it was he who should be pitied. God does not enter into a discussion with Elijah. As a result, Elijah witnesses a tremendous display of God's power, *"...a great and strong wind rent the mountains, and brake in pieces the rocks before the LORD..."* (verse 11), followed by an earthquake and a fire. He had already seen these divine demonstrations of power from the brook Cherith, Zarephath and Mount Carmel. However, the Lord was not in the wind, the earthquake or the fire. They were not the means of God's self-revelation.

INNER HEALING

At this time the Lord revealed His inexhaustible and inconceivable love to Elijah, *"...and after the fire a still small voice. And it was so, when Elijah heard it, that he wrapped his face in his mantle, and went out, and stood in the entering in of the cave"* (verses 12-13). Elijah left all the darkness of self-justification behind, and walked into the bright light of the love of God. This love conquered him and set him free of self pity. Now he was able to enter into the mystery. Eight hundred years later on the Mount of Transfiguration, Elijah and Moses spoke with the Son of God, *"...of his decease which he should accomplish at Jerusalem"* (Luke 9:31). Once again the restored servant stood before his God and was given new tasks.

CARRIED TO HEAVEN INSTEAD OF A PROPHET'S TOMB

"And it came to pass, when the LORD would take up Elijah into heaven by a whirlwind, that Elijah went with Elisha from Gilgal" (2nd Kings 2:1). This was a very interesting, yet unusual situation. The man who prayed under the juniper tree for the Lord to take his life did not experience death! Instead, he was taken up to heaven by a whirlwind. Elijah could have rightly said, "Dear God, thank You for not answering my prayer." God had other plans for him. It is good that God does not always answer our prayers! We often pray foolishly, short-sightedly, selfishly, and not in alignment with His will.

Elijah said, *"Lord, they have killed thy prophets, and*

digged down thine altars; and I am left alone, and they seek my life. But what saith the answer of God unto him? I have reserved to myself seven thousand men, who have not bowed the knee to the image of Baal" (Romans 11:3-4). While the Lord is honored and glorified through His Church, we must also remember that the Church is comprised of saved sinners with human limitations and weaknesses.

CHAPTER 10

PAUL: My Strength In Your Weakness

"...there was given to me a thorn in the flesh, the messenger of Satan to buffet me, lest I should be exalted above measure. For this thing I besought the LORD thrice, that it might depart from me. And he said unto me, My grace is sufficient for thee: for my strength is made perfect in weakness. Most gladly therefore will I rather glory in my infirmities, that the power of Christ may rest upon me."

2nd Corinthians 12:7-8

Perhaps the most dramatic conversion documented in the Bible is that of Saul of Tarsus. A zealous Jew involved in a sect known as "The Way," Saul persecuted and murdered Christians until his breathtaking conversion, which is recorded in the book of Acts.

The story of Paul (as Saul was named after his conversion) picks up a thread of thought that's woven through the accounts of the biblical characters we've already discussed. That intrinsic message is this: even the heroes of faith, whom we tend to put on pedestals where they don't belong, reached points at which they threw up their hands and cried, "I can't do this anymore!" This demonstrates to believers the human qualities of each of these men, reveals God's goodness to His children and illustrates God's sovereignty. The Lord answers prayer solely for His glory– regardless of whether we are Paul, Elijah, Jonah or Job.

In Paul we see an example of a very human characteristic: the infirmity or ailment that the apostle suffered with, *"...there was given to me a thorn in the flesh, the messenger of Satan to buffet me...For this thing I besought the Lord thrice, that it might depart from me"* (2nd Corinthians 12:7-8). Paul prayed to the Lord regarding a certain personal matter, but his prayers were not answered. The Bible does not disclose exactly what Paul's "thorn in the flesh" was, but it afflicted him so deeply that he prayed that God might deliver him from it. Apparently Paul thought that he could serve the Lord more effectively without this weakness. How many times have we said, "If

I was only feeling better I'd read my Bible," or "If I didn't have this physical ailment I would evangelize more aggressively"? Was the apostle suffering from a lack of faith? Did he not pray and fast enough? Was there a reason why God did not answer him? No. The apostle put his personal experience on a completely different level.

THE PRESERVING BLOWS

In his second letter to the church in Corinth, Paul wrote, *"...lest I should be exalted above measure through the abundance of the revelations, there was given to me a thorn in the flesh, the messenger of Satan to buffet me, lest I should be exalted above measure"* (2nd Corinthians 12:7). Previously, he wrote of a man who was *"caught up to the third heaven."* Fourteen years prior he heard *"unspeakable words, which it is not lawful for a man to utter."* The thorn in Paul's flesh (his cross) kept the apostle dependent on the Lord and not on his experiences. Notice how he said, *"there was given to me."* Pride and conceit can easily take hold of a blessed instrument of the Lord and bring about his downfall. That is one of the reasons why the Lord gives us preserving limitations and weaknesses. What would present-day prophets and miracle workers have done with this revelation?

THREE PRAYERS--NO DELIVERANCE

The apostle clearly stated that he *"besought the Lord thrice"*, he prayed once - no answer, he prayed again - no

163

answer. Only after the third prayer did the Lord answer, but not with deliverance. Let us remember that while God may not always answer our prayers the way we want, He has promised, *"There hath no temptation taken you but such as is common to man: but God is faithful, who will not suffer you to be tempted above that ye are able; but will with the temptation also make a way to escape, that ye may be able to bear it"* (1st Corinthians 10:13). We must acknowledge that His thoughts and ways are greater than ours. The same apostle who was entrusted with such great revelation is targeted by a messenger of Satan, but continued to work and live with a painful affliction.

SUFFERING TEACHES US TO PRAY

James, the brother of the Lord, offers this basic advice, *"Is any among you afflicted? let him pray"* (James 5:13). When we experience physical or mental suffering, we may confidently turn to the Lord. In this way we bring the Lord Himself into our personal distress. In turn the Lord will either choose to heal us, improve our situation, strengthen us, or maybe just leave things as they are. In all cases, the Lord does all things for His glory and our good.

From this perspective, we see that every form of suffering activates our prayer life, bringing us closer to the Lord. The Potter works on the clay and forms it as He will; we are transformed. We can give thanks for such times because the Lord has new blessings in store for our prayer lives.

THE ALL-SUFFICIENT GRACE OF GOD

Paul's letter clearly indicates that he had no intention of taking any glory in the revelations given him. Notice that when writing to the Corinthians, he uses the third person grammatical element instead of the first. Paul would rather glory in weakness because the Lord heard his prayer in a way other than what he expected, *"And he said unto me, My grace is sufficient for thee: for my strength is made perfect in weakness. Most gladly therefore will I rather glory in my infirmities, that the power of Christ may rest upon me"* (2nd Corinthians 12:9).

How does this happen in practical terms? It happens through the Holy Spirit who dwells in the hearts and lives of all believers. The exalted Lord knew best what was good for His apostle. The Lord did not remove his affliction, but He gave His servant the strength necessary to endure it. God's grace triumphs over the thorn in his flesh. Strengthened by the all-sufficient grace of God, the apostle can also say in effect, "Dear God, thank You for not answering my prayer." The Lord did not answer Paul's three prayers for deliverance; nevertheless, he achieved victory through grace.

Paul had already spoken of the glory of the New Covenant in his epistle and emphasized, *"But we have this treasure in earthen vessels, that the excellency of the power may be of God, and not of us"* (2nd Corinthians 4:7). Through this *"thorn in his flesh"* the apostle came to a deeper knowledge of the wonderful power of God which is made perfect in weakness.

Look at the Church and consider the vessels through

which the Lord has done His work. Without exception, we are weak, afflicted men and women who glory in His grace alone. Like Paul, the missionary to the Gentiles, we too *"...can do all things through Christ which strengtheneth me* (us)*"* (Philippians 4:13).

OF GOOD COURAGE

Consider the heart-wrenching testimony of the apostle, *"Therefore I take pleasure in infirmities, in reproaches, in necessities, in persecutions, in distresses for Christ's sake: for when I am weak, them am I strong"* (2nd Corinthians 12:10).

In his letter to the Romans, the apostle says that he and his co-workers, as messengers of Jesus, are *"...accounted as sheep for the slaughter,"* and before this he lists *"...tribulation, or distress, or persecution, or famine, or nakedness, or peril, or sword"* (Romans 8:35). He continues, *"...in all these things we are more than conquerors through him that loved us"* (Romans 8:37).

The risen Christ calls to every church, *"He that overcometh...."* How can we do this? Through Him who loved us through His finished work on the cross, and through His present ministry as our great High Priest at the right hand of God. Let us take advantage of this in faith and give Him the glory. Then grace will triumph over all weakness in our lives as well.

EUROPE IN FOCUS

At the apostles' council at Jerusalem, important resolutions were passed regarding the development of the early Church; namely, whether the Gentile Christians had to become Jews (keeping the law of circumcision, the Sabbath and dietary laws) in order to be saved. The apostles and elders who gathered together decided that Gentile Christians were equally saved by grace alone. Peter said, *"But we believe that through the grace of the Lord Jesus Christ we shall be saved, even as they"* (Acts 15:11). James agreed with this completely and, out of consideration for the Jews offered this advice, *"For Moses of old time hath in every city them that preach him, being read in the synagogues every sabbath day"* (Acts 15:21). In other words, Christians should abstain from certain things so they would not be an offense. Then a letter was sent to the young churches informing them of the resolutions passed by the council.

CHURCH GROWTH

Paul and Silas made it their task to visit the churches founded on Paul's first missionary journey, and inform them of the unanimous resolution passed in Jerusalem. Luke records the results of this ministry, *"And so were the churches established in the faith, and increased in number daily"* (Acts 16:5). Their journey took them through Syria, Cilicia and then to the province of Asia, where at Lystra they enlisted Timothy as a co-worker. He had already proven his worth in the local churches, and years later the apostle Paul was able to recommend him to the Christians in Philippi, *"For I have no man likeminded, who will naturally care for your state. For all seek their own, not the*

*things which are Jesus Christ's. But ye know the proof of him,
that, as a son with the father, he hath served with me in the
gospel."* (Philippians 2:20-22).

GUIDANCE THROUGH THE HOLY SPIRIT

After the missionary team had visited all of the existing
churches, they moved farther north. Unquestionably, Paul
and Silas prayed for guidance in their endeavors, but
twice experienced the Holy Spirit stopping them in their
tracks: "Do not preach here and do not preach there! Not
in the north and not to the west at Mysia." Where should
they go? Ultimately they came to the port of Troas. Before
them was the Aegean Sea and behind them the province
of Asia where they were not allowed to work. What now?
After weeks of prayer Paul heard the call in the night,
"Come over into Macedonia, and help us" (Acts 16:9).

Today we can say with all our hearts, "Dear God, thank
You for not answering Paul's prayers, and sending him and
his companions to Europe (Macedonia) instead." Because
of this the Gospel first came to Philippi. What happened
here was really dramatic. Lydia was the first woman to be
converted in Europe, demons were exorcised, Paul and
Silas were imprisoned and liberated by God through an
earthquake, and the prison guard was converted. This
church continued to support the apostle with their prayer
and gifts. Paul indeed was a testimony to God's providence,
the answer to his prayers were not decisive, but God's will
and purpose for his life was the determined factor of Paul's
service.

CHAPTER 11

DAVID: Lessons In Faith

"I will love thee, O LORD, my strength. The LORD is my rock, and my fortress, and my deliverer; my God, my strength, in whom I will trust; my buckler, and the horn of my salvation, and my high tower. I will call upon the LORD, who is worthy to be praised: so shall I be saved from mine enemies"

Psalm 18:1-3

As the second and greatest king of Israel, David led a very interesting life. For the most part, he was considered a man after God's own heart. He sought the Lord in all things as evidenced by the Psalms.

Born in Bethlehem, David was the youngest of Jesse's eight sons. In his youth, David was a shepherd credited with the courageous act of slaying Goliath, the great Philistine. As a result of this demonstration of bravery, King Saul had David brought into the court as an armor-bearer and musician.

Like a scarlet thread, the expressions, *"sought the face of the Lord...spoke before the Lord...called upon the Lord..."* are woven throughout David's life.

After his great fall, David confessed in Psalm 51:5, *"Behold, I was shapen in iniquity; and in sin did my mother conceive me."* All of us can relate to David in that while he did sin, he also experienced the restoring grace of God.

When we consider David, we should not overlook what he said of his life shortly before his death, *"...As the LORD liveth, that hath redeemed my soul out of all distress..."* (1st Kings 1:29).

David's life was rich in trials and tribulation, he was led on paths that demanded the utmost of him, but he continually experienced the timely and powerful help of the Lord.

Imagine what would have happened had he remained a shepherd with his father! Obviously his life would have been in conformity with the other shepherds who lived at that time in the fields of Bethlehem, but we would have known nothing about him. However, David was chosen by the Lord, anointed and set apart to be king over Israel.

Notice that the anointing as king took place in one day in the house of his father Jesse; however, the preparation for his service took years, and his proving another 40 years. The sequence is the same with our conversion. It is the event of a single moment of time, but sanctification is a life long process. In other words, growth follows birth, discipleship follows the calling. Therefore, it is worth looking into the life of David. May the Lord bless each reader throughout the course of this study.

DAVID'S YOUTH

As we mentioned, David was the youngest in the house of Jesse. His great grandparents were Ruth and Boaz. David had seven older brothers and two sisters. His name means the "beloved." The meaning of his name was fulfilled in various ways during the course of his life. It is obvious that David was loved by his parents. It was not by chance that Jesse entrusted his flock of sheep to him and gave him important tasks. We also learn that David had many friends, and was loved by Michal, the daughter of King Saul. However, he was loved much more by the Lord, the One who knows our hearts. Through Samuel He prophesied of him, *"...the LORD hath sought him a man after his own heart, and the LORD hath commanded him to be captain over his people"* (1st Samuel 13:14). Why him? Because David responded to the love of God with love. In Psalm 18:1, David said, *"I will love thee, O LORD, my strength."* David loved because the Lord loved him first.

David is an example that we should purpose to follow.

MUCH RESISTANCE BEFORE THE BATTLE

David was a shepherd. The shepherd's staff and sling were part of the standard equipment at that time; therefore, David must have learned how to use a sling at an early age.

We become better acquainted with David during the battle between Israel and the Philistines. Upon reaching the army, David first had to overcome the resistance of his three older brothers; Eliab, Abinadab and Shammah, who accused him of having false motives although he had come on the orders of his father.

It is just the same today. There are many "brothers" who, in the face of enemy threats, discourage and criticize the few individual warriors who confront the enemy in the name of the Lord.

When David relayed his victorious battles with a bear and a lion to King Saul, the king pointed out that he would have to confront the Philistine properly armed. Obeying Saul's orders, David put on the armor. He was not used to wearing this clumsy, awkward gear so he took it off and opted for the weapon he was more comfortable with during his years as a shepherd.

DAVID AND THE GIANT PHILISTINE

How did David overcome Goliath? In his shepherd's clothing, armed with a staff, a sling and a stone from the nearby stream. Was that all it took to defeat the giant? There can be no doubt that David prayed before this remarkable duel. Apparently David clung to the fact that Israel's wars were the Lord's wars. *"Then said David to the Philistine, Thou comest to me with a sword, and with a spear, and with a shield: but I come to thee in the name of the LORD of hosts, the God of the armies of Israel, whom thou hast defied. This day will the LORD deliver thee into mine hand; and I will smite thee, and take thine head from thee; and I will give the carcases of the host of the Philistines this day unto the fowls of the air, and to the wild beasts of the earth; that all the earth may know that there is a God in Israel. And all this assembly shall know that the LORD saveth not with sword and spear: for the battle is the LORD'S, and he will give you into our hands"* (1st Samuel 17:45-47).

How could this young shepherd boy have such confidence in the face of the mocking giant? Because he did not look at what was visible but, in accordance with Exodus 15:3, he trusted the invisible God of Israel.

We too must never forget the words James wrote under the inspiration of the Holy Spirit, *"Draw nigh to God, and he will draw nigh to you"* (James 4:8). We can "throw" our Word of God-based prayers at the enemy and strike him. We can fight from the finished victory of Jesus by standing our ground in faith.

RELIGIOUS UPBRINGING

We can certainly agree that the words of Proverbs 22:6 were fulfilled in David's upbringing, *"Train up a child in the way he should go: and when he is old, he will not depart from it."* David's parents obviously obeyed what the Lord commanded through Moses regarding child rearing, *"...and thou shalt teach them diligently unto thy children, and shalt talk of them when thou sittest in thine house, and when thou walkest by the way, and when thou liest down, and when thou risest up"* (Deuteronomy 6:7).

Jesse and his wife taught David the laws and ordinances concerning the worship of God. We can also see the godly influence of Boaz and Ruth, who undoubtedly prayed for their descendants. Their prayers were answered in David. His genealogy lists the male members of his ancestors from Judah to Jesse, but only a few female members are mentioned. For instance, we do not know David's mother's name. However, the powerful ministry of Samuel contributed to the fact that young David would later chose *"...the good and the right way"* (1st Samuel 12:23b). He learned the power of intercession and the Word of God from Samuel. Surely he heard of "Ebenezer," Israel's victory over the Philistines in answer to Samuel's prayers and the repentance of the people. As a refugee, David first sought shelter with Samuel at Rama. So we may presume that he had a reverent affection for the aged Samuel, the last judge and a great man of God.

THE ANOINTING OF A SHEPHERD BOY

Anointing David as king over Israel in Bethlehem under the mistrusting eyes of their ejected King Saul was a dangerous venture, so God instructed Samuel how to go about it. When the seven sons came before him one by one, Samuel must have thought that each was the right one, but from God's perspective, none of the seven young men were eligible for such service. The Lord said to Samuel, *"...Look not on his countenance, or on the height of his stature; because I have refused him: for the LORD seeth not as man seeth; for man looketh on the outward appearance, but the LORD looketh on the heart"* (1st Samuel 16:7).

The time had come, preparations had been made for the ceremony that would take place in Jesse's home, the only one missing was David, who was in the field tending the sheep. *"And he sent, and brought him in. Now he was ruddy, and withal of a beautiful countenance, and goodly to look to. And the LORD said, Arise, anoint him: for this is he. Then Samuel took the horn of oil, and anointed him in the midst of his brethren: and the Spirit of the LORD came upon David from that day forward. So Samuel rose up, and went to Ramah"* (1st Samuel 16:12-13).

Not only did the Lord give the commission, but He also supplied the necessary equipment. The apostle Paul wrote, *"For ye see your calling, brethren, how that not many wise men after the flesh, not many mighty, not many noble, are called: But God hath chosen the foolish things of the world to confound the wise; and God hath chosen the weak things of the world to confound the things which are mighty; And base things of the world, and things which are despised, hath God chosen, yea, and things which are not, to bring to nought things that are: That no flesh should glory in his presence"* (1st Corinthians 1:26-29).

SPECIAL TRAINING AT THE KING'S COURT

At first everything was great. King Saul took David to his court at Gibea. One of the court servants testified, *"...Behold, I have seen a son of Jesse the Bethlehemite, that is cunning in playing, and a mighty valiant man, and a man of war, and prudent in matters, and a comely person, and the LORD is with him"* (1st Samuel 16:18).

Today this would be considered making a career: no longer was David a shepherd boy; instead, he was privileged with the high calling to serve in the king's residence with his harp and songs. David wasn't just anyone in the king's court, he was Saul's bodyguard, *"And David came to Saul, and stood before him: and he loved him greatly; and he became his armourbearer"* (1st Samuel 16:21).

THE FATEFUL ERROR

Saul knew two sides of David, but there was another side of him that he did not know. Saul knew David as the one who brought him refreshment with his harp when he was troubled, and he knew him as a helper who bore his armor, but he never knew him as the redeemer of the nation. By which of these three characteristics do we know Christ?

Under the burden of a guilty conscience, King Saul was plagued with fear and trembling. His courtiers saw that he was suffering and advised, *"Let our lord now command thy servants, which are before thee, to seek out a man, who is a cunning player on an harp: and it shall come to pass, when the evil spirit from God is upon thee, that he shall play with his hand, and thou shalt be well"* (1st Samuel 16:16). Saul took their advice and brought David into his court to serve the king in this manner, *"And it came to pass, when the evil spirit from God was upon Saul, that David took an harp, and played with his hand: so Saul was refreshed, and was well, and the evil spirit departed from him"* (verse 23). This evil spirit came from the Lord who gave Saul over to the power of this spirit as punishment for his disobedience and rebellion.

The advice from Saul's servants was effective. The music from the harp and the spiritual songs from the gifted singer brought Saul refreshment. He always felt better afterward and the evil spirit departed from him. King Saul loved David because of the mental refreshment he received from his music. As a result, Saul showed him royal favor by employing David as his armor-bearer.

THE CONSEQUENCE OF SELF-DECEPTION

Doesn't this seem like a true picture of present-day Christianity? You might ask anyone on their way to church where they are going and he or she will likely answer, "I am going to church to worship. I always feel better after listening to the songs, and hearing the Word of God preached, it clears all my bad thoughts and makes me feel better." Well, that may be true, but what condition is your soul in? Many people will respond that they will do the best they can and when they can do no more, or they are confronted with a bad situation, they will call on Christ to "help" them. That is really the state of our self-sufficient society, isn't it? It takes too much humility to bow the knee to Christ, and our society reinforces the fact that we can do anything as long as we put our mind's to it. But the consequence of self-deception is hell. Things that make you feel good, and are generally accepted as good are not necessarily the will of God. Remember, the devil believes in God too, but he trembles.

ALONE IN THE VALLEY OF DEATH?

We have already established the fact that David's music soothed the king, but the whole scene is about to change! The Philistines gathered for battle, assembling their entire army in the valley of Elah. David stood at Saul's side as his armor-bearer in the valley of the giant. No amount of harp music would bring refreshment to him at a time like this! The only thing Saul heard was the mocking laughter of the enemy, *"When Saul and all Israel heard those words of the Philistine, they were dismayed, and greatly afraid"* (1st Samuel 17:11).

Do you remember prior to your salvation, when all a church service meant was an uncertain absolution for an overburdened conscience? How many times did we say, "I'll handle it myself!" Do you remember how terrible it was to come home from a comforting church service and be confronted with reality, the giant in the valley of the shadow of death? You trembled with fear. Neither the gentle spiritual organ music nor the beautiful hymns of the choir will refresh or help you in this valley. A mocking Satan stands before you as your accuser. An army of sins were before your eyes, but you did not know Him. You were alone in the dark valley of death. Even if all those who, like you, were deceived by Satan were to stand with you, none of them would be able to help you.

Not a single man in Israel's army could (or would) stand up to the giant of Gath. *"And all the men of Israel, when they saw the man, fled from him, and were sore afraid"* (1st Samuel 17:24). No one could help Saul in this battle.

Let's praise the Lord that we no longer see Christ as just a harpist or armor-bearer, but as the Redeemer of our souls. For those who only seek Christ occasionally, the day will come when they, like Saul will have to meet the giant. No one will be there to help them unless they have truly believed that God's anointed was the perfect Savior!

CAPTAIN OVER A THOUSAND

Having already discussed David's battles with a bear and a lion, it is relevant that we now read about his service under King Saul, *"And David went out whithersoever Saul sent him, and behaved himself wisely: and Saul set him over the men of war"* (1st Samuel 18:5). *"And Saul was afraid of David, because the LORD was with him"* (verse 12). And *"...he went out and came in before the people. And David behaved himself wisely in all his ways; and the LORD was with him"* (verses 13-14). *"Then the princes of the Philistines went forth: and it came to pass, after they went forth, that David behaved himself more wisely than all the servants of Saul"* (verse 30). Because the Lord was with His anointed one, he was a very wise and successful leader of thousands. Likewise, if the Lord is with us, we will enjoy success in all we do.

But David's success did not help Saul in his sin. Jealousy of David turned Saul into an enemy, *"And the women answered one another as they played, and said, Saul hath slain his thousands, and David his ten thousands. And Saul was very wroth, and the saying displeased him; and he said, They have ascribed unto David ten thousands, and to me they have ascribed but thousands: and what can he have more but the kingdom?"* (1st Samuel 18:7-8).

SAUL SETS A CUNNING SNARE

King Saul promised David the hand of his oldest daughter Merab. This was a promise in which Saul would not keep. Saul used the budding love of his younger daughter, Michal, to set a snare for David. The king didn't demand a dowry, but rather a hundred foreskins of the Philistines, *"...to be avenged of the king's enemies."* However, his ulterior motive was *"...to make David fall by the hand of the Philistines"* (1st Samuel 18:25).

When David fulfilled the king's demand in double measure, Saul gave him his daughter Michal to be his wife. However, that didn't stop his perseverance, nor his bitter unrepentant attitude. *"And Saul saw and knew that the LORD was with David, and that Michal Saul's daughter loved him. And Saul was yet the more afraid of David; and Saul became David's enemy continually"* (1st Samuel 18:28-29).

JONATHAN'S UNIQUE FRIENDSHIP

While King Saul fell into a deeper depression and his life became consumed with envy and jealousy toward David to the point he wanted to kill him on several occasions, his eldest son (and candidate for the throne) reacted quite differently. Jonathan saw his savior in David. David was sent by God and had liberated Israel from the power of Goliath. Following David's victory over Goliath, the Bible says, *"Then Jonathan and David made a covenant, because he loved him as his own soul. And Jonathan stripped himself of the robe that was upon him, and gave it to David, and his garments, even to his sword, and to his bow, and to his girdle"* (1st Samuel 18:3- 4).

These words show us two things: 1) Jonathan loved David, and 2) he humbled himself. Why did Jonathan love David so much? Because he realized that David had gone into battle for him and risked his life. From that hour on, his heart belonged to David. Not only did he see the work David accomplished and through which he was saved, but his eye and heart saw Him who accomplished the work. It wasn't enough for him to know that Goliath was dead and Israel was free, but his whole being was attracted to the person who had liberated him. It wasn't that he thought little of the victory, but to him, the victor was more important.

WHAT IS OUR RELATIONSHIP TO OUR SAVIOR?

Shouldn't we also open our hearts to the One who bought us at such a cost? Why are our hearts often so cold toward the Savior? Is it because He and His work are so seldom before our eyes? The Lord said to His disciples, *"Behold my hands and my feet"* (Luke 24:39). Do we behold them? What do the pierced hands and feet of our Savior say to us? Don't they express to us that He hung on the cross and bore our judgment?

Jonathan is a fitting example of the sacrificial love that exalts the beloved one! Why did he strip himself of his robe, garments, sword, bow and girdle? Because David was everything to him. This self-sacrifice not only shows us how great the person of David was to him, but also how completely he entered into the victory of David. What did his weapons—which expressed honor, dignity and power—mean to him after David's accomplished victory? He no longer needed his armor because David had beaten the enemy. These things may have been valuable to him at one time, but what use were they to him now that he was united with David? All honor and power belonged to David alone.

David's heart must have rejoiced over this genuine friendship and devotion. What about us? Do we cause the heart of our Lord to rejoice because of our devotion? How easily are we satisfied with our salvation, while we leave Him who accomplished it in the background? Certainly we should rejoice over our salvation, but should our hearts stop at salvation? Shouldn't it be as it was with Jonathan and Paul? Shouldn't we dedicate all that we value to Him, and exalt Him who went to His death for us?

In the days that followed, Jonathan proved the genuine nature of his friendship with David on several occasions.

We may experience misunderstanding and rejection in our own families, but we need not feel defeated or alone if we are wholly on the side of Him who experienced more rejection than we will ever know!

VOLUNTARY DEVOTION

David did not demand Jonathan's devotion, nor does the Lord demand it from us. Our devotion must come from the source of love. Jonathan forgot himself and thought only of David. It should be the same for us if Christ dwells in our hearts.

This exemplary form of devotion is also found in the apostle Paul. As valuable as his own righteousness had once been, he spoke these profound words after the Lord saved his soul, *"But what things were gain to me, those I counted loss for Christ. Yea doubtless, and I count all things but loss for the excellency of the knowledge of Christ Jesus my Lord: for whom I have suffered the loss of all things, and do count them but dung, that I may win Christ"* (Philippians 3:7-8).

THE REFUGEE IN THE SCHOOL OF SUFFERING

The stories of David's flight are like a great adventure.

When David and Saul met for the last time, David put his pursuer to shame by saying, *"...the king of Israel is come out to seek a flea, as when one doth hunt a partridge in the mountains"* (1st Samuel 26:20). Remember, David had fallen from the highest ranks of Saul's court to the deepest pit of a homeless refugee. At first he stood alone.

How could God have allowed this to happen? Why didn't He answer David's prayer and free him from this suffering? David adhered to that which Abigail said to him, *"Yet a man is risen to pursue thee, and to seek thy soul: but the soul of my lord shall be bound in the bundle of life with the LORD thy God..."* (1st Samuel 25:29).

David knew that his life was in the strong hand of the One who anointed him as king. He clung to the fact that the Lord of hosts would not only determine the beginning, but also the end of his sufferings under King Saul.

THE PRAYER OF GROWING TRUST

"And Saul sought to smite David even to the wall with the javelin; but he slipped away out of Saul's presence, and he smote the javelin into the wall: and David fled, and escaped that night. Saul also sent messengers unto David's house, to watch him, and to slay him in the morning: and Michal David's wife told him, saying, If thou save not thy life to night, to morrow thou shalt be slain" (1st Samuel 19:10-11). The pressure was increasing and the clouds of darkness gathered on the horizon. Had Saul drowned the first signs of jealousy in a sea of prayer this story would have had a

much different ending!

Think about how dreadfully dangerous those days must have been for David! Saul's hatred caused him to leave his own house. David did not voluntarily walk out on his family, he was forced to flee. He knew of no sin in his life that could have caused such an attack, *"For, lo, they lie in wait for my soul: the mighty are gathered against me; not for my transgression, nor for my sin, O LORD"* (Psalm 59:3).

When we find ourselves in similar situations, we can learn how to overcome such adversity through David's trials. If you notice how David confronted this increasing pressure you will understand why God allows clouds of darkness to gather over us.

David begins this psalm by casting himself upon God in order to find liberation in Him. From a feeling of total helplessness, he prayed himself into a peaceful trust and a song of victory. This occurred despite the fact that his situation had not changed, the enemy was still lying in wait for him. In desperation he cried out to the Lord for physical salvation. Snares and resistance awaited him everywhere, but David escaped the terror and found peace in the Lord.

MOMENTARY AFFLICTION

David knew that every night of affliction and tribulation must come to an end, *"...weeping may endure for a night, but joy cometh in the morning"* (Psalm 30:5). God does not allow the enemy to test us beyond our limits. Sometimes joy may not come the next morning, but it never comes too late!

INWARDLY IN GREAT DANGER

During his flight from Saul, David approached Ahimelech the priest at Nob. Ahimelech was shocked when he saw David alone and in the typical haste of someone who is fleeing. David wanted to eat something quickly and then continue his flight. To allay the suspicions of the priest, he told a "white lie." He said that King Saul had sent him on an urgent secret mission. He only came to him to refresh himself. Then David asked Ahimelech if he could give him a weapon. Ahimelech gave him the sword of Goliath and David fled to Achish, the king of the Philistines. It was there that he was recognized, but pretended to be mad so that he would not be killed. Here we witness the inner decline of a believing man. Consider these three points:

1) It began with a lie

In order not to arouse suspicion, David told Ahimelech, "...*The king hath commanded me a business, and hath said unto me, Let no man know any thing of the business whereabout I send thee, and what I have commanded thee: and I have appointed my servants to such and such a place*" (1st Samuel 21:2). God does not tolerate lies.

2) Grasping at fleshly weapons

The decline continued. First David lied to Ahimelech,

now he sought a weapon. David acted much differently when he battled Goliath, He rejected Saul's armor and fought in the name of the Lord with his sling. This time he asked the priest for a spear or sword to protect himself from Saul's wrath. David's attitude in the battle with Goliath was more admirable because he did not put his trust in weapons or armored protection, but relied solely on the Lord.

How quick do we resort to weapons, human help, wisdom and experience when we should take refuge in Christ alone?

3) Listening to people

David's behavior toward Achish shows that his faith was decreasing. He pretended to be insane, relying on the superstition of the Philistines who would not dare kill such people out of fear that the spirits from their bodies might attack them.

In his youth David was not afraid of Goliath; however, when he was confronted by a much weaker Achish, David feared for his life. Why? He heard what the highest officers told their lord of him and how they warned him, *"Is not this David the king of the land? did they not sing one to another of him in dances, saying, Saul hath slain his thousands, and David his ten thousands?"* (1st Samuel 21:11). And David *"...laid up these words in his heart, and was sore afraid of Achish the king of Gath"* (1st Samuel 21:12). David took human words to heart, instead of trusting in the Word and promises of God which is why he became confused and fearful. When we take the Word of God to heart–listening to or reading it–fear of man will be driven from us.

How did this inward decline come about? During his flight from Saul, David only thought of saving his own life. He no longer took time to commune with God, who had predestined him to be king. Instead, his fear controlled his thinking and led him to believe that the matter was in his own hands and he needed to protect his life. Apparently it hadn't occurred to him that this would have been a good time to call upon the Lord.

How often do we do this? The momentary stress or distress seems so urgent that we feel like we cannot "lose" any time in prayer. The only way we are going to experience victory over all the hectic unrest of everyday life is by hearing the Word of our God and communicating with Him through prayer.

DAVID COMES TO KNOW HIS HOMELAND

Continuing on his flight from King Saul, David hid in caves at Adullam and En-Gedi (Psalm 57 and 142). God had not answered his prayers regarding Saul's relentless pursuit, but through his flight the Lord gave him the advantage of travelling around the country he would later rule. Without understanding the purpose, he came to know the various regions of the land and its soil, the agriculture and livestock, crafts and trade, and the needs of his future subjects. From this perspective, all of those years of flight were not in vain, but a necessary preparation for the throne in Jerusalem.

SAFETY IN A FOREIGN COUNTRY?

For fear of their safety, David brought his parents to the Moabites. Through the mouth of the prophet Gad, the Lord said to David, *"...Abide not in the hold; depart, and get thee into the land of Judah. Then David departed, and came into the forest of Hareth"* (1st Samuel 22:5-6).

We can only imagine that David was tired of being on the run and wanted to lead a normal life again with his family; however, God had other plans. Although David didn't realize it at the time, God was preparing him for rulership through these various trials.

Child of God, remember, if you are going through many trials, don't run away, be still, because the Lord wants to purify, smooth and polish you through these difficult times. The Potter is working on the clay, forming it, so that it will become a useful vessel.

Later on David returned to King Achish in Gath suffering from a severe bout of depression. The Bible says, *"And David said in his heart, I shall now perish one day by the hand of Saul: there is nothing better for me than that I should speedily escape into the land of the Philistines; and Saul shall despair of me, to seek me any more in any coast of Israel: so shall I escape out of his hand"* (1st Samuel 27:1). In this instance the servant forgot to seek the counsel of his heavenly Master. Certainly the God of Israel could protect him from Saul in the Promised Land! We are all in danger of seeking fast human solutions to our trials instead of enduring until the Lord has done with us as He has chosen.

FLIGHT FROM GOD

Why do people choose to flee from God when they are confronted with various persecutions and tribulation? Tortured with a guilty conscience or a broken heart we seek to remedy the problem in our own strength while remaining inwardly empty and restless. Some resort to various forms of psychotherapy, while others run from one pleasure to another. It is in these trying times that we forget that the Maker of heaven and earth is beyond capable of coming alongside of us to either fix our problem, heal our heart or give us the strength to go forward. Blessed are those who have fled to Jesus during those trying times!

DAVID'S KINGSHIP - LESSONS IN LEADERSHIP

The end of David's persecution by Saul came when the king was killed, *"So Saul died, and his three sons, and his armourbearer, and all his men, that same day together"* (1st Samuel 31:6). David's reaction to the deaths of Saul and Jonathan are surprising. We can easily understand why David would mourn the loss of Jonathan, but that same sorrow of loss is also communicated toward the man that threatened to take David's life, *"And David lamented with this lamentation over Saul and over Jonathan his son"* (2nd Samuel 1:17). David's response gives us a very clear look into his heart. Although Saul had tormented him in every possible way, David did not harbor any resentment, but left it to the Lord to resolve this painful conflict. Right up to the very end, David considered Saul to be the Lord's anointed one. He praised the men of Jabesh-Gilead who buried Saul and his two sons. In doing so, David could now begin the next phase of his life without any burden or guilt.

It is only to our advantage when we conduct an inner evaluation from time to time by praying like David, *"Search me, O God, and know my heart: try me, and know my thoughts: And see if there be any wicked way in me, and lead me in the way everlasting"* (Psalm 139:23-24). Ask the Lord to show you whether you are harboring any negative feelings in your heart against your brother or sister. Forgiveness and reconciliation keep our lives free of things which interrupt our connection with the Lord. Many people forget this and walk around with unforgiven sin or a gnawing bitterness in their hearts.

CONTACT WITH HEAVEN

The difference between Saul and David was that Saul's actions were in vain. He didn't consult God before he did anything, and everything he did do was for his own selfish gain. On the other hand, David, for the most part, sought guidance and direction from the Lord, *"And it came to pass after this, that David enquired of the LORD, saying, Shall I go up into any of the cities of Judah? And the LORD said unto him, Go up. And David said, Whither shall I go up? And he said, Unto Hebron"* (2nd Samuel 2:1). David was a man of prayer who did not want to take a step without the Lord's leading.

BEGINNING AT HEBRON

Before Caleb conquered the city of the Anakims (giants), it was called Kirjath-arba. Abraham had stayed at nearby Mamre, where he bought a piece of land to be used as a family burial plot. Hebron, approximately 927 meters (2,825 feet) above sea level and the highest city in Israel is situated 30 kilometers (18 miles) southwest of Jerusalem.

While Abner was the captain of the army, the ten tribes of Israel initially clung to the house of Saul, and made Ish-bosheth, Saul's son, successor. However, the men of Judah anointed David as king over them in Hebron. The battles between the house of Saul and the house of David lasted for years.

KING OVER ISRAEL

More blood was shed even after Joab murdered Abner. Two leaders of the bands of soldiers killed Ish-bosheth–who had been completely helpless since the death of Abner–while he was sleeping. Then finally, the tribes not belonging to Judah did what they should have done long ago, they anointed David as king over all of Israel. The hour had come for David to liberate Jerusalem from the hand of the Jebusites.

JERUSALEM BECOMES THE CAPITAL

In 1996 the city of Jerusalem celebrated her 3,000th anniversary. According to our understanding, David's men conquered the Jebusite city 1,004 years before Christ. When the king and his army came to Jerusalem, the Jebusites mocked, "*...Except thou take away the blind and the lame, thou shalt not come in hither: thinking, David cannot come in hither*" (2nd Samuel 5:6). "*And David said on that day, Whosoever getteth up to the gutter, and smiteth the Jebusites, and the lame and the blind, that are hated of David's soul, he shall be chief and captain. Wherefore they said, The blind and the lame shall not come into the house. So David dwelt in the fort, and called it the city of David. And David built round about from Millo and inward*" (2nd Samuel 5:8-9).

This was truly a historical hour! The site of the future temple and the throne of David were at last in the hands of Israel! The necessary preparations had been made in order for this prophecy to be fulfilled. The Lord Jesus called the city, "*...the city of the great King*" (Matthew 5:35). Jerusalem was greatly contested then as it is today. We are witnessing the preparations for the last chapter of spiritual history to be completed; namely, the building and culmination of the Church, the Rapture and the Day of the Lord for Israel and the nations.

THE ENEMY TARGETS THE SHEPHERDS

Soon after David was anointed king over Israel, the

Philistines mobilized their armies, *"But when the Philistines heard that they had anointed David king over Israel, all the Philistines came up to seek David"* (2nd Samuel 5:17). The Philistines figured that if they could get the shepherd (King David) then they could get the sheep (the people). This offers a practical lesson that applies to our lives. The enemy has made pastors (the shepherd's of God's people) his special target. If he can bring about the fall of one, he can do much damage to a church or Christian institution. Let us pray for the protection of our pastor's in this delicate role that they have been called to.

THE KING USES THE WEAPON OF PRAYER

While the Philistines attacked twice, we also read that David inquired of the Lord twice, *"And David enquired of the LORD..."* (2nd Samuel 5:19 and 23). David had not forgotten who Israel's highest commander was who had led them in war. He did not hold war councils with his captain Joab and his officers, but took refuge in prayer. We can learn a valuable lesson in prayer from David's example.

First, David experienced a wonderful answer to his prayers. The Lord encouraged him to attack the Philistines, and that which He promised David came to pass. In memory of the victory, the place was called "Baal-perazim" or "the Lord who breaks out." But the Philistines were stubborn. Apparently they were not affected by their first defeat because they made another attempt. David did not make the mistake that we so often make by simply repeating the strategy since it worked so well the first time. Instead, he again sought guidance from the Lord, who gave the following instructions, *"...Thou shalt not go up; but fetch a compass behind them, and come upon them over against the mulberry trees. And let it be, when thou hearest the sound of a going in the tops of the mulberry trees, that then thou shalt bestir thyself: for then shall the LORD go out before thee, to smite the host of the Philistines"* (2nd Samuel 5:23-24). David demonstrated that not only was he a hearer of the Word, but he was also a doer, *"And David did so, as the LORD had commanded him..."* (2nd Samuel 5:25). Trusting prayer and obedient action led to two significant victories over the enemy. From this we learn three important steps in maintaining our victory.

1. David stood upon the Word of God

Not only did David receive the assurance of divine help prior to his calling, but prior to these victories, he also received the expressed assurance that God would establish his throne forever (7:13). We find repeated confirmation of this covenant in the Psalms. Additionally, at this particularly successful venture against Edom came the special promise that Edom/Esau would be subject to his brother Israel/Jacob (Genesis 27:40). Whoever stands on the solid ground of the Word, is founded on the promises of God and possesses an army which cannot be beaten.

2. David experienced God's help

Those who stand on the Word of God have God's help and will experience the fulfillment of His promises. We read of the results of David's obedience in 2nd Samuel 8:6 and 14, *"And the LORD preserved David whithersoever he went."* This invisible protection was infinitely superior to all the visible enemies who confronted David. No Philistine, Moabite, Syrian or Edomite could overcome it. It was not David's military genius or the bravery of his soldiers that guaranteed the victory, but the hand of God which intervened from above. Blessed are those who have this hand of protection! In Jesus Christ we know that God is for us. So we may well ask, "who can be against us?" (Romans 8:31 onward). The Lord Himself wages the battle while His servants help to build His kingdom. Therefore all the glory belongs to Him and never to the instrument (His people) He uses.

3) David had the people of God behind him

For seven years David was recognized as king of Judah. Now, however, all of Israel stood united with him. What a host! Yes, they were sinful people, but they were people of the covenant nevertheless. David had not subdued this people by force, but waited patiently for God to place them under his rule. Now that all of Israel was behind him, he experienced victory upon victory.

Whoever relies upon the Word of God enjoys His protection, and untainted fellowship with His people, victory in his church and work.

GRATEFUL RETROSPECT

The king sat in his palace at Jerusalem. All of the surrounding nations had either been conquered or were on friendly terms with Israel. David could now focus his attention on other tasks. He had time to play his harp and sang songs of victory and praise. The introduction of Psalm 18 says, "A Psalm of David, the servant of the LORD, who spake unto the LORD the words of this song in the day that the LORD delivered him from the hand of all his enemies...." When we read this glorious psalm, we see why David was considered a man after God's own heart. David, in contrast to King Saul, saw himself as God's servant through whom the Lord could exercise His rule over Israel. He ruled in complete dependence upon the heavenly government.

David looks back and gives us a glimpse of his prayer life and even lets us take part in it, *"I will call upon the LORD, who is worthy to be praised: so shall I be saved from mine enemies...In my distress I called upon the LORD, and cried unto my God: he heard my voice out of his temple, and my cry came before him, even into his ears"* (verses 3 and 6). David "called" and "cried", he did not sit in a warm room and recite a formal prayer, he was in mortal danger, *"The sorrows of hell compassed me about: the snares of death prevented me"* (Psalm 18:5). He then describes the Lord's mighty intervention, *"Then the earth shook and trembled; the foundations also of the hills moved and were shaken, because he was wroth. There went up a smoke out of his nostrils, and fire out of his mouth devoured: coals were kindled by it"* (verses 7-8).

Doesn't this remind you of Revelation 8 where John saw how the prayers of the saints produced voices, thunder and lightning, and an earthquake? Our prayers have included us in spiritual history and the governments of the world.

David continues to describe the Lord's help, *"He sent from above, he took me, he drew me out of many waters. He delivered me from my strong enemy, and from them which hated me: for they were too strong for me...He brought me forth also into a large place"* (verses 16-17 and 19). In spite of many things he did not understand, he sang, *"As for God, his way is perfect: the word of the LORD is tried: he is a buckler to all those that trust in him. For who is God save the LORD? or who is a rock save our God?...Therefore will I give thanks unto thee, O LORD, among the heathen, and sing praises unto thy name. Great deliverance giveth he to his king; and sheweth mercy to his anointed"* (verses 30-31 and 49-50). Do we use such words when we pray? Do we sing songs like this?

AN EXEMPLARY TESTIMONY

Successors to the throne in Jerusalem were measured by God according to their ancestors. We've all heard the saying, "Like father, like son." Unfortunately this was true of only a few of David's descendants, the so-called "reformatory" kings. Regarding most of them, the Lord said, *"...and have not walked in my ways, to do that which is right in mine eyes, and to keep my statutes and my judgments, as did David his father"* (1st Kings 11:33).

The apostle Paul referred to the Lord's words in 1st

Samuel 13:14, while at a synagogue at Antioch in Pisidia, *"...he raised up unto them David to be their king; to whom also he gave testimony, and said, I have found David the son of Jesse, a man after mine own heart, which shall fulfil all my will"* (Acts 13:22).

PREPARATIONS FOR THE TEMPLE

Nathan was a true servant of the Lord who carried out His Word fearlessly. King David spoke to him about his heart's desire (a matter about which he had doubtlessly also prayed), to build a house for the Lord because he himself lived in a house of cedar, while the ark of the covenant was still in a tent. When Nathan heard David's plan, he encouraged him and thought he was definitely the right man in God's eyes to build a temple in Jerusalem. For many years David collected the necessary materials for the future temple. He said, *"Now I have prepared with all my might for the house of my God the gold for things to be made of gold, and the silver for things of silver, and the brass for things of brass, the iron for things of iron, and wood for things of wood; onyx stones, and stones to be set, glistering stones, and of divers colours, and all manner of precious stones, and marble stones in abundance"* (1st Chronicles 29:2).

NATHAN'S MESSAGE IN THE NIGHT

Evidently God had a different plan. The following night God told His servant His thoughts concerning

David, his descendants and the building of the temple in Jerusalem. He desired to build a house for the God of Israel but God's thoughts were higher than David's. Through Nathan He said, *"...Shalt thou build me an house for me to dwell in? Whereas I have not dwelt in any house since the time that I brought up the children of Israel out of Egypt, even to this day, but have walked in a tent and in a tabernacle"* (2nd Samuel 7:5-6). Although God said no to David's prayer, He said, *"...thou didst well in that it was in thine heart"* (2nd Chronicles 6:8). Can you imagine how encouraging this comment was for David? It would certainly make a lasting impression in his life!

The Lord reminded David of the blessing that had been imparted to him to that point. But then through Nathan He said, *"...the LORD telleth thee that he will make thee an house"* (2nd Samuel 7:11b). David wanted to build the Lord a house of stone; instead, the Lord would build a house for David, *"And thine house and thy kingdom shall be established for ever before thee: thy throne shall be established for ever"* (2nd Samuel 7:16). The Lord also made the following promise to Abraham, *"...and kings shall come out of thee"* (Genesis 17:6), and of Sarah He said, *"...I will bless her...and she shall be a mother of nations; kings of people shall be of her"* (verse 16). The Lord also said to Jacob at Bethel, *"...I am God Almighty...and kings shall come out of thy loins"* (Genesis 35:11). Judah, the great-great-grandson of Abraham, was given the express promise that a leader would come from him, *"The sceptre shall not depart from Judah, nor a lawgiver from between his feet, until Shiloh come; and unto him shall the gathering of the people be"* (Genesis 49:10).

FULFILLED AND UNFULFILLED PROPHECY

These verses are a good example of a part of the Old Testament in which some things are fulfilled in the near future while others are fulfilled in a much more distant future. Solomon was the next descendant, he built the temple in Jerusalem. When the Babylonians captured Jerusalem in 587 B.C., the time of the nations began. David's throne in Jerusalem no longer existed. However, when the Lord Jesus returns, He will seat Himself on the throne of David.

KINGLY WORSHIP

David worshipped God when he heard that through his family would come a divine descendant and king. He addressed God six times with the words, *"O LORD God,"* and ten times he humbly called himself His servant. Before the Israelites he was a victorious king, but before God He was a servant, *"...there is none like thee, neither is there any God beside thee, according to all that we have heard with our ears"* (2nd Samuel 7:22). Apparently David understood the extent of his election which is clearly indicated in Psalm 2:7-8, *"I will declare the decree: the LORD hath said unto me, Thou art my Son; this day have I begotten thee. Ask of me, and I shall give thee the heathen for thine inheritance, and the uttermost parts of the earth for thy possession."*

How does a child of God react when his or her prayers are not answered? Let us learn from David. He did not lament over God's denial for him to build the temple. He rejoiced over the promise of future blessings, and acknowledged God's sovereignty. Let us not forget that God will not fulfill all of our desires, but He will fulfill all of His promises.

THE ORGANIZATION OF WORSHIP

Together with Zadok and Ahimelech, the king divided the sons of Aaron into 24 orders (1st Chronicles 24) who were responsible for the worship of God in the temple. He also appointed 24,000 Levites, *"for the service of the house of the LORD."* This was the *"purifying of all holy things, and the work of the service of the house of God"* (1st Chronicles 23:28). *"Moreover four thousand were porters; and four thousand praised the LORD with the instruments which I made, said David, to praise therewith"* (1st Chronicles 23:5).

David was not only a psalmist and singer himself, but he was also responsible for organizing the music in the temple, *"And David spake to the chief of the Levites to appoint their brethren to be the singers with instruments of musick, psalteries and harps and cymbals, sounding, by lifting up the voice with joy"* (1st Chronicles 15:16).

SONG FOR TEMPLE DEDICATION

Psalm 30:1 is introduced with the words, "A Psalm and Song at the dedication of the house of David." The contents of this psalm show that David wrote it after he had sinned by numbering the people, and after he had purchased the threshing place of Araunah the Jebusite (2nd Samuel 24, 1st Chronicles 21:1-22:1) as land for the temple.

SINGERS PRAISE GOD

In various books of the Old Testament we repeatedly come across the words, *"...to praise the Lord according to the order of David, the king of Israel."* The 24 orders of Levites were formed under David's rule, led by Asaph, Heman and Juduthun (1st Chronicles 25). Twice in this chapter we come across the words, *"...according to the order of the king"* (verses 2 and 6). David gave the royal command to praise the Lord. Two hundred and eighty-eight trained singers (as we would call them today) had the glorious task of praising God in His temple.

INSPIRED BUILDING PLAN

In the same way God showed Moses the exact plan for the tabernacle on Mount Sinai, so too He gave David exact instructions for building the temple. At the dedication of the tabernacle we read, *"...as the Lord commanded Moses."* Why? Because God specifically told Moses, *"According to all that I shew thee, after the pattern of the tabernacle, and the pattern of all the instruments thereof, even so shall ye make it"* (Exodus 25:9 and 40). It was imperative that the earthly sanctuary of God corresponded with the heavenly sanctuary, right down to the last detail.

David gave Solomon, his son and successor, the exact pattern of the temple with the words, *"All this...the LORD made me understand in writing by his hand upon me, even all the works of this pattern"* (1st Chronicles 28:19). Surely David must have explained to Solomon the various stages of the building of the temple and the temple court with great emotion, *"...and the pattern of all that he had by the spirit"* (verse 12). Then he encouraged Solomon with the words, *"Take heed now; for the LORD hath chosen thee to build an house for the sanctuary: be strong, and do it...Be strong and of good courage, and do it: fear not, nor be dismayed: for the LORD God, even my God, will be with thee; he will not fail thee, nor forsake thee, until thou hast finished all the work for the service of the house of the LORD"* (1st Chronicles 28:10 and 20).

VOLUNTARY COLLECTION

It is very refreshing to read about the generosity of the *"...chief of the fathers and princes of the tribes of Israel, and the captains of thousands and of hundreds, with the rulers of the king's work...Then the people rejoiced, for that they offered willingly, because with perfect heart they offered willingly to the LORD; and David the king also rejoiced with great joy"* (1st Chronicles 29:6 and 9).

In his prayer of thanksgiving, David reminds us that we should be faithful stewards of all that the Lord has entrusted to us. Moreover, he directs our eyes to our own mortality, so that we may create things of eternal value.

DAVID'S GREATEST FALL

We know from Scripture that David was a man after God's own heart, but he was still a man with a sinful nature equally capable of falling into various temptations. Through several avenues Satan capitalized on David's weaknesses. Weapons, pride, riches and sex have brought about the downfall of many of the Lord's servants. David fell prey to the whispering enemy in the scandal with the wife of his faithful officer Uriah and in numbering the people. Scripture does point out the fact that the devil lurked behind these evil deeds, *"And Satan stood up against Israel, and provoked David to number Israel"* (1st Chronicles 21:1).

DAVID'S FALL TOOK PLACE IN THREE STAGES

1. Dangerous love of comfort

The rainy winter season was over and the war against the Ammonites resumed; however, David remained in Jerusalem. Was he tired from the long war? Did he think they could win this war without him? Those who keep their distance from the battle must hear the words of judgment, *"Now therefore the sword shall never depart from thine house"* (2nd Samuel 12:10). The very thing David wanted to stay away from now came upon him in an increased measure. There would be strife and bloodshed in his own house. He wanted to avoid the disturbance of war, yet he brought disturbance into his very own house and heart.

The backsliding of many Christians begins with the sin of loving their comfort zone. Suddenly they resent the long way to the places where they found inner strength from the Word of God. They make themselves comfortable and withdraw from God's holy war. We gain nothing when we leave the work in the Church and the mission field to others.

2. Limitless Lust

David probably could have avoided his second mistake had he kept his eyes in control. But he saw the beautiful Bathsheba and lusted after her, prompting his damaging downward spiral. The sin of lust and a lack of discipline also brought about Samson's fall. Let us beware of the first look, the arising lust, and let us flee immediately by turning our eyes and thoughts upon the Lord. How many servants of the Lord have fallen because of lust and desire? May God keep us pure!

"But every man is tempted, when he is drawn away of his own lust, and enticed. Then when lust hath conceived, it bringeth forth sin: and sin, when it is finished, bringeth forth death" (James 1:14-15). Let us use David as our example and guard our thoughts.

3. Shameless Dishonesty

When we fall into sin, the next step is always dishonesty; we lie to try and cover up our actions. David's conversation with Uriah sounds very innocent. He called the officer back and asked him how things were going in the front and suggested he spend a few days at home with his wife in the hopes of hiding the disgrace that Bathsheba was expecting his child. When this plan failed as a result of Uriah's exemplary discipline, he sent a letter to Joab containing a death sentence for the Hittite. So we see that one sin leads to another, David had now become tangled in a web of sin!

REPENTANCE AND RESTORATION

How can we lead people to the way of repentance today? Let us consider three points:

1) The goodness of God

David was reminded of God's love in his life up to that point, as well as the many manifestations of His grace. *"...Thus saith the LORD God of Israel, I anointed thee king over Israel, and I delivered thee out of the hand of Saul...and gave thee the house of Israel and of Judah; and if that had been too little, I would moreover have given unto thee such and such things"* (2nd Samuel 12:7-8). The Lord had wonderfully led David and was prepared to add further blessings.

Therefore the vision of God's undeserved favor should lead the sinner to repentance. The apostle to the Gentiles raised the following question in Romans 2:4, *"...despisest thou the riches of his goodness and forbearance and longsuffering; not knowing that the goodness of God leadeth thee to repentance?"*

What things God has done for those who resist His call even up to the present day! How many times has He confronted them with His Word and shown them much grace in inner and outer distress? Can pointing this out to rebellious people awaken their conscience and touch their hearts?

2) The sin of man

After Nathan pointed out the amount of grace God had shown David during his life he asked, *"Wherefore hast thou despised the commandment of the LORD, to do evil in his sight? thou hast killed Uriah the Hittite with the sword, and has taken his wife to be thy wife..."* (2nd Samuel 12:9). Nathan then proceeded to list David's sins: despising the commandment of the Lord, adultery, murder. Against the radiant background of God's unmerited grace, the darkness of David's sins became more and more prominent.

Is the list of our sins shorter than David's? We know from Jesus' Sermon on the Mount how seriously God takes sin. Jesus said that if we look upon another with lust in our hearts, we have committed adultery, and if we utter hateful words against our brother we are a murderer...so, is our list of sins shorter than David's?

3) Nathan revealed God's goodness and David's guilt

Then he points to God's wrath and judgment and advised David of the nature of the punishment appointed by God, *"Now therefore the sword shall never depart from thine house...Thus saith the LORD, Behold, I will raise up evil against thee out of thine own house..."* (verses 10-11).

Continual war, misfortune and disgrace in his own family was what King David had to look forward to. Our God is a holy God, a consuming fire. Not only must we convey that message to unbelievers, but we must never lose sight of it ourselves. God takes sin seriously.

The reference to God's goodness and wrath, combined with the ingratitude and sin of man led David to repentance, *"I have sinned against the LORD"* (verse 13, compare also Psalm 51:32). Only God's grace and subsequent restoration could bring about a new beginning in David's life. May the word of the Lord spoken through His prophet bring many to repentance.

Why was David's prayer for his child not answered? God pardoned David for his sin and allowed him to live, *"...The LORD also hath put away thy sin; thou shalt not die"* (2nd Samuel 12:13). However, David's sin would not go unpunished, *"Howbeit, because by this deed thou hast given great occasion to the enemies of the LORD to blaspheme, the child also that is born unto thee shall surely die"* (verse 14). Doesn't this appear to be a limitation of God's grace? Sometimes our limited intellect only understands grace as a means of escaping punishment, but biblical grace is more than that. Biblical grace takes the eternal punishment of God's judgment away, but it does not always remove the results and consequences of sin. The grace of God allowed David's child, who was conceived in sin, to die.

Let's take a closer look into why God allowed this to happen:

1) This rod of correction was necessary on account of God's enemies. Through the child's death, those who had

mocked with their mouths were silenced. They were able to see that the God of Israel does not treat sin lightly, He is holy and righteous. If no sign of judgment had accompanied grace, many people would have a false sense of security in believing that God does not take sin so seriously.

2) This could have been dangerous for David as well. Think about it. If God had allowed the child to live, David might not have realized how gravely he had sinned. He might have become complacent in his worship of the Lord thinking that he could do whatever he wanted and not experience any consequences. As believers we love the Lord, but we must also fear Him. David would have forgotten that had everything always turned out "his way."

This situation kept David humble and sensitive to his sin and aware of his complete dependence on God. Verse 16 paints a moving portrait of David's reliance on the Lord, *"David therefore besought God for the child; and David fasted, and went in, and lay all night upon the earth."* This new distress kept David in close contact with his God, and his prayer life remained alive and intact.

3) The Lord allowed the child to die on the seventh day (verse 18). David did not bury himself in his grief but acknowledged God's heavy, exalted hand upon him. Immediately following the child's death, David went to the sanctuary where he worshipped God for His divine guidance (verse 20). It is there that God comforted him and he was able to move on.

David's behavior is a moving testimony. Many people may have thought that because David's child was dead that God did not treat the godly any different from the godless. But this situation and the way David handled himself illustrated the tremendous difference between the child of God and the child of the world.

May God also help us have such an attitude when we experience sorrow.

CHASTENING GRACE

When the believer falls into sin he is chastised by the Lord. When you are on the receiving end of divine discipline it is difficult to glory in it, but that is when we should rejoice because God's Word tells us that the Lord will chasten those He loves. This is really good news! For those who struggle with their salvation or feel forsaken by God, remember this promise. God has no reason to chastise the unbeliever. Think of it this way: As a parent or adult, you do not have the liberty of disciplining somebody else's children. In the same way, the unbeliever belongs to this world, led by the prince of darkness...they are somebody else's children!

Consider these verses which testify to the good that comes from being chastened by God, *"...For they* (our fathers) *verily for a few days chastened us after their own pleasure; but he for our profit, that we might be partakers of his holiness."* And, *"Now no chastening for the present seemeth to be joyous, but grievous: nevertheless afterward it yieldeth the peacable fruit of righteousness unto them which are exercised thereby"* (Hebrews 12:10-11, compare also Titus 2:11 onward). As we have just stated, children of God experience His chastening because, *"...if ye be without chastisement, whereof all are partakers, then are ye bastards, and not sons"* (Hebrews 12:8).

In spite of David's failures, he remained a man after God's own heart because of the way in which he bore God's chastening. How did David behave after God forgave him? Let's take a look at one instance: Pressure from Absaloms' rebellion caused David to leave Jerusalem. Weeping, he walked barefoot with his head covered up the Mount of Olives. He endured the cursing of Shimei the Benjaminite of the house of Saul as a part of God's chastisement (2nd Samuel 15:30 and 16:5 onward). Are we practiced in the school of the Lord? Can we resist His chastening? Can we harden our hearts against it yet continue to call ourselves Christians?

THE ROYAL PSALMIST

Of all the Old Testament books, the Psalms most clearly describe the faith of the individual believer in the Lord. The Psalms are the inspired answers of the hearts of men to God's revelation of Himself in history, prophecy and the Law. Throughout the course of time the saints have used this collection of prayers and praise in their services and for their personal worship.

When we consider this we are reminded of C.H. Spurgeon's *The Treasury of David.* What a tremendous blessing this interpretation of the 150 psalms has brought to Christianity. Seventy-three psalms were written by David and two by Solomon. The majority of the psalms were written 1,000 years before Christ. We'll conclude this chapter with 12 important points that relate to David and ourselves:

1) To pour our hearts before God, making everything into a prayer, *"When thou saidst, Seek ye my face; my heart said unto thee, Thy face, LORD, will I seek"* (Psalm 27:8).

2) To claim the Lord's promises by basing our prayers on the Word of God. David came into the presence of the Lord on the grounds of Deuteronomy 4:29, *"But if from thence thou shalt seek the LORD thy God, thou shalt find him, if thou seek him with all thy heart and with all thy soul."*

3) To examine ourselves to see whether we are praying like David (with all our hearts and souls rather than with just our minds). Are our prayers empty or are they a cry from our hearts? Do we pray earnestly or habitually? Do we pray with words we have memorized or with the words the Lord puts on our hearts?

4) To, like David, have the Lord before us who knows everything, sees everything and is omnipresent, *"O LORD, thou hast searched me, and known me. Thou knowest my downsitting and mine uprising, thou understandest my thought afar off"* (Psalm 139:1-2).

5) To hold fast to the omnipotence and sovereignty of God, trusting in His infinite power and help?

6) To rejoice over His Word when we read or hear it. **David uses various pictures to describe what the Word**

meant to him, *"The law of the LORD is perfect, converting the soul: the testimony of the LORD is sure, making wise the simple. The statutes of the LORD are right, rejoicing the heart: the commandment of the LORD is pure, enlightening the eyes. The fear of the LORD is clean, enduring for ever: the judgments of the LORD are true and righteous altogether. More to be desired are they than gold, yea, than much fine gold: sweeter also than honey and the honeycomb. Moreover by them is thy servant warned: and in keeping of them there is great reward"* (Psalm 19:7-11).

7) To praise, worship and adore Him as David did in Psalm 9:2 and 11, *"I will be glad and rejoice in thee: I will sing praise to thy name, O thou most High...Sing praises to the LORD, which dwelleth in Zion,* and Psalm 34:1, *"I will bless the LORD at all times: his praise shall continually be in my mouth."*

8) To trust in the grace of God alone, and rejoice over the forgiveness we have experienced, *"Blessed is he whose transgression is forgiven, whose sin is covered"* (Psalm 32:1).

9) To long for the leading and teaching of the Lord exemplified by David in Psalm 5:8, *"Lead me, O LORD, in thy righteousness because of mine enemies; make thy way straight before my face,"* and Psalm 25:4-5, *"Shew me thy ways, O LORD; teach me thy paths. Lead me in thy truth, and teach me: for thou art the God of my salvation; on thee do I wait all the day."* David was convinced of the truth of Psalm 25:12, *"What man is he that feareth the LORD? him shall he teach in the way that he shall choose."*

10) To know that we are safe by day and night in the hand of the Lord. David said, *"I laid me down and slept; I*

awaked; for the LORD sustained me" (Psalm 3:5). And, *"I will both lay me down in peace, and sleep, for thou, LORD, only makest me dwell in safety"* (Psalm 4:8).

11) To have the blessed assurance that the Lord hears our prayers, *"I cried unto the LORD with my voice, and he heard me out of his holy hill"* (Psalm 3:4). *"I sought the LORD, and he heard me, and delivered me from all my fears...This poor man cried, and the LORD heard him, and saved him out of all his troubles"* (Psalm 34:4 and 6)

12) To have a vision for the Lord's claim to the whole world, *"But the LORD shall endure for ever: he hath prepared his throne for judgment. And he shall judge the world in righteousness, he shall minister judgment to the people in uprightness"* (Psalm 9:7-8).

THE HEAVENS DECLARE THE GLORY OF GOD

"The heavens declare the glory of God; and the firmament sheweth his handywork" (Psalm 19:1).

"O LORD our LORD, how excellent is thy name in all the earth! who hast set thy glory above the heavens" (Psalm 8:1).

"When I consider thy heavens, the work of thy fingers, the moon and the stars, which thou hast ordained; What is man, that thou art mindful of him? and the son of man, that thou visitest him?" (Psalm 8:3-4).

David exclaimed these truths in reverence and wonder. He who had spent time as a young shepherd in the fields of Bethlehem had learned from his youth not to rely on his own capabilities, but to cry out to the Lord. This was very often a great help to him. The Psalms are full of such cries for help and praises he experienced.

David followed the Lord as a servant and could have rightly said in the end, "Dear God, thank you for not answering my prayer." Why? Because it was not the answer to his prayers that were decisive, what mattered most was the Lord Himself, for He is the answer to all things!

Conclusion

It must be presumed the reader has understood that the primary purpose of this book is to focus our attention on seeking the will of God. We are followers of Jesus, not of self. Consider Jesus' testimony in John 6:38, *"I came down from heaven, not to do mine own will, but the will of him that sent me."* These were not idle words, but words of such substance that it involved life and death. Prior to His arrest, Jesus prayed the following words in the Garden of Gethsemane, *"not my will, but thine, be done"* (Luke 22:42).

Of course, one of the most effective ways we have to discern God's will for our lives is by maintaining an active prayer life which is based not on receiving the answers we desire, but on developing an understanding of God's plan for us. Those of us who are parents have said the word "no" to our children countless times. Would a father who loves his child hand him a book of matches? Denying potentially harmful requests – which as parents we are obligated to – doesn't mean that we will deny our child every request thereafter. What a sad relationship it would be if a child suddenly stopped asking his parents for certain things just because he feared the answer would always be no. This reminds us of our relationship with our heavenly Father: If God does not answer our prayers immediately, or the way we have asked, should we stop praying? Absolutely not.

The Word of God urges us to pray: *"I exhort therefore, that, first of all, supplications, prayers, intercessions, and giving of thanks, be made for all men"* (1st Timothy 2:1).

Jesus encouraged His followers with these words, *"Ask, and it shall be given you; seek, and ye shall find; knock, and it shall be opened unto you"* (Matthew 7:7). In Matthew 26:41 He implored His disciples to *"Watch and pray, that ye enter not into temptation."* Innumerable examples throughout Scripture exhort us to spend time in prayer. As a matter of fact, our Lord Himself spent entire nights in prayer, *"he went out into a mountain to pray, and continued all night in prayer to God"* (Luke 6:12). Prayer is our lifeline to God and is evidence of our living faith in the Lord Jesus.

This book was also written in an effort to clear up some misconceptions of certain passages of Scripture regarding our new life in Christ. In general, a newly converted person is illustrated as one who has broken bad habits and passions and is now experiencing a joyful life; one whose marriage has been restored and whose children have miraculously begun obeying their parents in virtually every respect.

You probably have yet to attend a church service where someone has stood up during a time of testimony and thanked God for allowing him or her to be ill. Can you imagine the reaction such a comment would receive? Such prayer diametrically opposes the general "Christians-are-always-happy-and-smiling" teaching often promoted today. Of course we have joy in being Christians, but we also experience a great deal of sadness, pain, suffering and loneliness–feelings that can lead to a full-fledged case of depression. That is the reality of the Christian life.

Addressing the Church, James encouraged them to bear suffering and affliction, *"Take, my brethren, the prophets, who have spoken in the name of the Lord, for an example of suffering affliction, and of patience. Behold, we count them happy which endure. Ye have heard of the patience of Job, and have seen the end of the Lord; that the Lord is very pitiful, and of tender mercy"* (James 5:10-11). Dieter Steiger has done a marvelous job in dealing with Job and his suffering in Chapter 7. Further, the apostle Peter wrote, *"Wherein ye greatly rejoice, though now for a season, if need be, ye are in heaviness through manifold temptations"* (1st Peter 1:6). Therefore heaviness, grief, suffering, sadness, difficulty, disappointment, and sorrow are part of our new life in Christ.

This biblical doctrine directly opposes today's modern gospel which promises happiness and a life full of joy. The Bible does not promise such a "happy, hallelujah, praise the Lord" life to the Christian. On the contrary, it condemns those who publicly teach that if you follow the Lord and contribute (generously) to their work, the Lord will bless you with health and wealth. These charlatans have crept into the Church and are proclaiming that the advantage of the flesh is spiritual gain. If that were true, why would Paul have written the following words to the church at Philippi,"*... many walk, of whom I have told you often, and now tell you even weeping, that they are the enemies of the cross of Christ.*" (Philippians 3:18). Paul lists the sufferings he endured for the sake of the Gospel: *"Are they ministers of Christ? (I speak as a fool) I am more; in labours more abundant, in stripes above measure, in prisons more frequent, in deaths oft. Of the Jews five times received I forty stripes save one. Thrice was I beaten with rods, once was I stoned, thrice I suffered shipwreck, a night and a day I have been in the deep; In journeyings often, in perils of waters, in perils of robbers, in perils by mine own countrymen, in perils by the heathen, in perils in the city, in perils in the wilderness, in perils in the sea, in perils among false brethren; In weariness and painfulness, in watchings often, in hunger and thirst, in fastings often, in cold and nakedness"* (2nd Corinthians 11:23-27).

Again, while addressing the Philippians, Paul wrote, *"Brethren, be followers together of me, and mark them which walk so as ye have us for an ensample"* (Philippians 3:17). If you are to follow Christ in the newness of life, you must heed the admonition of the great apostle Paul, who invites the believer to follow him because his motive is directed to Jesus.

Do you want to follow Jesus? Then follow the instruction Jesus gave through Paul. What was Paul's desire? How did he want his new life to be exemplified? **What was his real goal?** The answers are found in verse

10, *"That I may know him, and the power of his resurrection, and the fellowship of his sufferings, being made conformable unto his death."* Doesn't this contradict what is being taught today? So often we hear the words, "Follow Jesus and you will be led out of suffering;" "Only in Him you will find the fullest expression of joy;" and "He will restore your life to an abundance." While these and other similar statements are biblical, they are not meant for the flesh. Paul, the great warrior for truth, proclaimer of the Gospel, and apostle to the Gentiles actually prayed to take part in *"the fellowship of his sufferings."*

My dear child of God, have you thanked the Lord for your physical infirmities yet? Have you told Him that you accept the sufferings from His hands? If not, then you have failed to recognize the direction in which Jesus wants to lead you.

Paul goes a step further: He actually prays that he would be *"made conformable unto his death."* These words clearly reveal the naked truth of our lives in the flesh. This precept doesn't correspond with the things of this world or other people, nor does it fit the proclamation, "Follow Jesus and you will change the world." Why not? Because no such promise has been given to us in Scripture. Jesus wants you to be willing and ready to lay down your life for Him. Are you ready? This life in the flesh has no future. This may seem difficult to understand, but it is the only way to follow the Lord.

Paul makes that clear when writing to the church in Rome, *"Knowing this, that our old man is crucified with him, that the body of sin might be destroyed, that henceforth we should not serve sin"* (Romans 6:6). So my question to you is this: "Is your life really crucified with Christ?" If so, then you are walking the narrow way, the way of loneliness and suffering, but confident in the promise, *"Rejoice in the Lord alway: and again I say, Rejoice"* (Philippians 4:4). This is a very private matter between you and the Lord. Following Jesus does not mean following Him in a crowd. Jesus is interested in you in a very personal way. He cares more for you than you can possibly imagine. The closer you come to Him the more often you will be able to pray, "Dear God, thank you for not answering my prayer."